Bev. – loves Meek? work on that.

THE SHADOW BOX

THE SHADOW BOX

MICHAEL CRISTOFER

DRAMA BOOK SPECIALISTS (PUBLISHERS)
NEW YORK

For my mother and father,
Mary and Joseph Procaccino

The Mark Taper/Long Wharf Theatre production of THE SHADOW BOX *was first presented on Broadway on March 31, 1977 by Lester Osterman, Ken Marsolais, Allan Francis and Leonard Soloway at The Morosco Theatre, New York City with the following cast:*

THE INTERVIEWER	Josef Sommer
COTTAGE ONE	
JOE	Simon Oakland
STEVE	Vincent Stewart
MAGGIE	Joyce Ebert
COTTAGE TWO	
BRIAN	Laurence Luckinbill
MARK	Mandy Patinkin
BEVERLY	Patricia Elliot
COTTAGE THREE	
AGNES	Rose Gregorio
FELICITY	Geraldine Fitzgerald

The play takes place in three cottages on the grounds of a large hospital.

Directed by Gordon Davidson
Setting by Ming Cho Lee
Lighting by Ronald Wallace
Costumes by Bill Walker

viii

Originally produced by Center Theatre Group of Los Angeles at the Mark Taper Forum.

THE SHADOW BOX *was awarded the Pulitzer Prize for Best Drama and the Antoinette Perry Award for Best Play in 1977.*

ACT ONE

Morning

A small cottage that looks like a vacation house, set in the trees, secluded. A front porch, a living room area and a large kitchen area.

The lights come up first on a small area downstage and away from the cottage. A stool is there. We will call this area the "Interview Area."

JOE is surprised by the light. He is a strong, thick-set man, a little bit clumsy with moving and talking, but full of energy.

He steps into the light and looks out toward the back of the theatre. A MIKED VOICE *speaks to him.*

VOICE OF INTERVIEWER   Joe? Joe, can you hear me?

JOE   Huh? (*Looking around*) What . . . uh . . . ?

VOICE OF INTERVIEWER   Can you hear me?

JOE   Oh, yeah. Sure. I can hear you real good.

VOICE OF INTERVIEWER   Good. Have a seat, Joe.

JOE   (*Still looking around, a little amused*) What? Hey, where . . . uh . . . I can't see . . .

VOICE OF INTERVIEWER   We're out here.

JOE   What? Oh, yeah. I get it.

VOICE OF INTERVIEWER   Yes.

JOE   You can see me. Right?

VOICE OF INTERVIEWER   Yes. That's correct.

JOE   You can see me, but I . . .

VOICE OF INTERVIEWER   Yes.

JOE   . . . can't see you. Yeah. (*He laughs*) I get it now. You can see me, huh?

VOICE OF INTERVIEWER   Yes, we can.

JOE   Far out.

VOICE OF INTERVIEWER   What?

JOE   (*Smiling*) Nothing. Nothing. Well, how do I look?

VOICE OF INTERVIEWER   Have a seat, Joe.

JOE   That bad, huh? I *feel* all right. Lost a little weight, but outside of that . . .

VOICE OF INTERVIEWER   Have a seat, Joe.

JOE   Sure. Sure. (*He sits*) Okay. What?

VOICE OF INTERVIEWER   Nothing special. We just wanted to talk. Give you a chance to see how we do this.

JOE   Sure.

VOICE OF INTERVIEWER   There's nothing very complicated about it. It's just a way for us to stay in touch.

JOE   Yeah. It's like being on TV.

VOICE OF INTERVIEWER   Just relax.

JOE   Right. Fire away.

VOICE OF INTERVIEWER   You seem to be in very good spirits.

JOE   Never better. Like I said, I feel great.

VOICE OF INTERVIEWER   Good.

        (*There is a pause.* JOE *looks out into the lights*)

JOE   My family is coming today.

VOICE OF INTERVIEWER   Yes. We know.

JOE   It's been a long time. Almost six months. They would have come sooner, but we couldn't afford it. Not after all these goddamn bills. And then I always figured I'd be going home. I always figured I'd get myself back into shape and . . . (*Pause*)

VOICE OF INTERVIEWER   Have you seen the cottage?

JOE   Yeah. Yeah, it's real nice. It's beautiful. They're going to love it.

VOICE OF INTERVIEWER   Good.

JOE   Maggie always wanted a place in the mountains. But I'm an ocean man. So, every summer, we always ended up at the beach. She liked it all right. It just takes her a while to get used to things. She'll love it here, though. She will. It's real nice.

VOICE OF INTERVIEWER   Good.

JOE   It just takes her a little time.

   (*The lights slowly start to come up on the cottage area.* MAGGIE'S *and* STEVE'S *voices are heard off stage*)

STEVE   Here. Over here.

MAGGIE   Stephen!

VOICE OF INTERVIEWER   (*To* JOE)   Then everything is settled, right?

JOE   What? Oh, yeah. Maggie knows the whole setup. I wrote to her.

VOICE OF INTERVIEWER   And your son?

JOE   Steve? Yeah. I told Maggie to tell him. I figured he should know before he got here.

VOICE OF INTERVIEWER   Good.

JOE   It's not an easy thing.

STEVE   (*Still off stage—overlapping*)   Come on, Mom.

JOE   I guess you know that.

MAGGIE   (*Still off stage*)   Give me a chance to catch my breath.

JOE   You get used to the idea, but it's not easy.

VOICE OF INTERVIEWER   You seem fine.

JOE   Oh, me. Yeah, sure. But Maggie . . .

MAGGIE (*Overlapping*)   What number did you say it was?

VOICE OF INTERVIEWER (*Overlapping*)   What number cottage are you in?

JOE   Uh . . . one. Number one.

STEVE (*Overlapping*)   Number one. One, they said.

JOE   You get scared at first. Plenty. And then you get . pissed off. Oh, is that all right to say?

VOICE OF INTERVIEWER   Yes, Joe. That's all right. It's all right for you to be angry or depressed or even happy . . . if that's how you _feel_. We want to hear as much as you want to tell us.

STEVE (*Still off stage*)   Look at all se goddamn trees!

MAGGIE (*Still off*)   Watch your mouth.

JOE   Yeah, 'cause I was. Plenty pissed off. I don't mind telling you that. In fact, I'm glad just to say it. You get tired of keeping it all inside. But it's like, nobody wants to hear about it. You know what I mean? Even the doctors . . . they shove a thermometer in your mouth and a stethoscope in their ears . . . How the hell are you supposed to say anything? But then, like I said, you get used to it . . . I guess . . .

STEVE   Come on, Mom!

JOE   There's still a few things . . .

MAGGIE   You're going to give me a heart attack.

JOE   I could talk to you about them . . . maybe later.

VOICE OF INTERVIEWER   Even if it's just to listen. That's what we're here for, Joe.

JOE   I mean, it happens to everybody, right? I ain't special.

VOICE OF INTERVIEWER   I guess not, Joe.

JOE   I mean, that's the way I figure it. We could talk about that, too.

VOICE OF INTERVIEWER Yes, we can.

JOE But maybe tomorrow.

VOICE OF INTERVIEWER All right, Joe. We won't keep you now.

JOE I'm a little nervous today.

VOICE OF INTERVIEWER But if you need anything . . .

JOE Huh . . . What . . . ?

VOICE OF INTERVIEWER If you need anything . . .

JOE Oh, sure. Thanks. We'll be all right.

VOICE OF INTERVIEWER You know where to find us.

JOE Is that it?

VOICE OF INTERVIEWER That's it. Unless *you* have something . . .

JOE Oh . . . yeah. One thing . . . I . . . uh . . .

STEVE (STEVE *is a young boy, about fourteen years old.*) Dad? (*He rushes onto the stage, runs around the cottage.*)

MAGGIE (*Still off stage*) Stephen?

STEVE Here! Over here!

JOE I . . . uh . . . no. No. I guess not.

VOICE OF INTERVIEWER All right, then. Thank you, Joe.

JOE Sure. Any time.

STEVE (*Rushing into the cottage*) Number one. This is it! Jesus!

JOE Oh, yeah. I want to thank you for making all this possible. (*He looks out into the lights. There is no answer.*) Hello?

STEVE He's not there.

JOE You still there? (*Still no answer*) Well, I'd better be getting back.

(*Still no answer. The lights fade on the Interview Area and come up full on the cottage.*)

STEVE (*Running out of the cottage*) Mom? Where the . . .

JOE (*Turning toward the cottage*) Stephen! Hey, dad!

STEVE Holy shit! Holy . . . ! (*He does a little dance, runs to his father and embraces him*) Where the hell . . .

JOE There you are . . . I been waiting all day.

STEVE . . . have you been? We been traipsing around the whole goddamn place . . .

JOE (*Laughing*) I been here. Waiting. Where's your mother?

STEVE One cottage after another. Is this it? Is this it?

MAGGIE (*Still off*) Joe? Stephen, is that your father?

STEVE Far out! I brought my guitar. Wait till you hear . . . (*Calling off*) Mom! Over here, for Christ's sake. (*To* JOE) So many goddamn trees . . .

JOE What do you think? Huh?

STEVE So many . . .

JOE There's a bunk in there.

MAGGIE (*Off*) Joe?

JOE Hey, Maggie. Get the lead out!

STEVE Yeah. I saw. Bunk beds and a fireplace . . . we got any wood?

JOE You can take the top one night and the bottom the next.

STEVE Uh-uh. I'll take the bottom. I fall off, I'll break my fucking head.

JOE I'll break your fucking head, if you don't watch your fucking mouth.

STEVE Holy, holy shit!

(STEVE *hugs his father again.*

    JOE *holds him at arm's length for a second, to catch his breath*)

STEVE You okay?

JOE (*Quickly recovers and returns to his previous level of energy*) Yeah, yeah, I'm great.

STEVE You look terrific. I was worried. I missed you. Hey! How long can we stay? Huh?

JOE I don't know. A couple of weeks . . . I don't know how long it . . .

STEVE Great. (*He drags* JOE *into the cottage*) Come on. I'll show you the guitar. It was pretty cheap. I ripped off the case, so that didn't cost anything. It's got a little compartment on the inside for picks and capos and dope and shit like that . . .

(*They go into the cottage.* MAGGIE *struggles onto the stage, a mass of bundles, shopping bags and suitcases. She's dressed up—high heels, bright yellow print dress—but she looks a mess. She's been walking too long, carrying too big a load. Finally, she stops near the cottage.*)

MAGGIE End of the line. Everybody off.

(*And she lets all the shopping bags, packages, and suitcases crash to the ground around her. She straightens her back with a groan and looks around her.*)

Steve? Joe? The jackass is here! Come and get your luggage?

(*No answer. She walks up to the porch of the cabin, and takes one step up. But the cottage seems to frighten her. She stops, looks at it and then backs away from it.*)

You leave me alone out here for one more minute and I'm taking the next plane back to Newark.

(*She gives out a long, loud whistle through her teeth.*)

Stephen, are you in there or not?

STEVE (*From inside the cottage*) Hey, Mom, come on in if you're coming.

MAGGIE   I'm not coming in. You're coming out. And
don't give me . . .

JOE (*Coming out of the cottage and saying her line with
her*) . . . and don't give me any smart back talk or
I'll split your lip.
> (*Surprised by* JOE's *sudden appearance, she
> doesn't move for a second. Then, very carefully,
> she takes a few slow steps toward him.* JOE *walks
> down to meet her. All* MAGGIE *can manage to do
> is reach out one hand and touch him, just to see if
> he's really there. When she is sure that he's not
> an illusion, she takes a deep breath, goes back to
> her bundles, and starts talking very quickly, try-
> ing to keep control of herself.*)

MAGGIE   Well . . . I brought you some things . . . I
didn't know what, what for sure you'd want, but I
thought it was better to be sure, safe . . . so . . .

JOE   We'll take them inside . . .

MAGGIE   No . . . Steve'll get them. I been dragging
them all . . .

JOE   Let me look at you, huh?

MAGGIE (*Continues to fumble nervously with her hair,
her dress, the packages*) I didn't know what you'd
need. There's some jelly and some peppers I put up
. . . (*She starts pulling jars out of one of the bags.*) I
thought it was forty pounds on the plane, but they let
you have extra. You can put things under the seat. A
lot of people didn't *have* anything, so I put stuff
under *their* seats, too.

JOE   How are you, Maggie?

MAGGIE   Oh, fine, I brought the newspapers. (*She
pulls more jars out.*) Some cookies, and some pump-
kin flowers. The airplane made me sick. There was a
man sitting next to me. He kept talking and talking.
All those clouds. It looked like you could walk on

them. I wanted to throw up, but the man next to me made me so nervous I couldn't. Where did I put . . .

JOE   Come on inside. You want some coffee?

MAGGIE   (*Reaching into another bag*) I brought some coffee. You've got everything here already. You should've told me.

JOE   I did. I told you over the phone.

MAGGIE   I don't remember. I'll clean up tomorrow. First thing. Straighten everything out.

JOE   It's already clean.

MAGGIE   You want to live in somebody else's dirt?

JOE   Maggie, it isn't the Poconos. It's clean. It's clean.

MAGGIE   Well, you can't be too sure. Mom sent some bread . . .

JOE   How is she?

MAGGIE   Oh good. Yeah. She fell down and hurt her leg. I don't know. It's not healing so good. She's getting old. What can you do. But she made the bread anyway. I told her not to, but she said she wanted to. So . . . And Fanny says hello. She gave me . . . uh, something . . . where is it? Oh, yeah. Here . . . (*She pulls out a wrapped package.*)

JOE   I can see it later.

MAGGIE   I don't know what it is. You know Fanny. It could be anything . . . and some clam broth. Oh, Pop and Josie, they went crabbing, they took the kids. Steve went with them. They gave me almost a whole bushel. So I made some sauce. (*Another jar emerges.*) We can . . . do you have a stove in there?

JOE   Sure. Come on inside. I'll show you. It's real nice. (*He starts to head her toward the cottage, but she pulls away.*)

MAGGIE   No, I don't want to go inside.

JOE   Huh? Why not?

MAGGIE I don't . . . I'll see it. I'll see it.

JOE But . . .

MAGGIE How do I look? It's a new dress.

JOE You look real pretty.

MAGGIE I got dressed for the plane. I don't know. I should have worn pants. You get so tired, sitting, all pushed together like that. My ears hurt so bad. Steve loved it. I couldn't make him sit still. He was all over the place, taking pictures. The stewardess was crazy about him. She was *pretty*, too. They look real nice. They wear . . . they smile. I asked her what to do about my ears and she just smiled. I don't think she heard me. So I smiled, too, but it didn't do any good . . .

JOE You must be tired, huh?

MAGGIE Yeah. I don't know.

JOE (*Hugs her*) Come on in. You can rest.

MAGGIE (*Ignores his offer*) One minute you're there. The next minute you're here. I still feel like I'm there. (*She pulls away from him and starts rummaging through the bags.*) What else? Three thousand miles, it must be. They . . . Oh, yeah. I made a ham . . . (*She pulls the monster out of a bag.*)

JOE What?

MAGGIE A ham. We can have it for lunch.

JOE Christ!

MAGGIE What's the matter? It's no good?

JOE You mean you carried a ham three thousand miles across the country?

MAGGIE No. I put it under the seat.

JOE Well, what the hell are we going to do with it?

MAGGIE I don't know . . . I thought it'd last, so . . .

JOE We *got* everything we need. I told you.

MAGGIE I don't remember. You can't eat this, huh?

JOE   No, I can eat it. I can eat it. That's not what I'm talking about.

MAGGIE   Then what *are* you talking about?

JOE   I'm talking about they got ham in California. They got stores like every place in the world and you go in and you buy whatever you want . . .

MAGGIE   (*Making a vain effort to hide the ham*)   I'll take it back with me . . .

JOE   It's all right! It's here now.

MAGGIE   (*Overlapping*)   It'll keep. I'll put it away. You don't have to look at it.

JOE   (*Overlapping*)   No. It's fine. It's all right. *What the hell are we talking about?!!*

MAGGIE   (*All upset, still holding on to the ham*)   You didn't say in the letter. And we talked and I couldn't remember. I tried. What the hell. They said to come and bring Steve. That's all. At first I thought that was it. Then I got your letter and you sound fine and I talk to you . . . so, I made the ham . . . I . . .

   (*She cries.* JOE *goes to her. Holds her and the ham in his arms*)

JOE   I missed you, Maggie. I missed you real bad.

MAGGIE   You got to tell me what's going on. Don't make me feel so stupid. Like I'm supposed to know everything. I don't know nothing. I just know what I see.

JOE   Maggie . . .

MAGGIE   But you look real good. You're all right now, huh?

JOE   Maggie, listen . . .

MAGGIE   No. It's all right. You don't have to tell me. I can see it. You're fine. Huh? It's just I got so scared. Thinking about it. Making things up in my head. But it's all right now. I can see it's all right. I knew it would be when I got here.

JOE (*Giving in*)   Yes, Maggie. Everything's all right.

MAGGIE   I knew it. I knew it.

> (*Our focus shifts now to the Interview Area.*
> BRIAN *is talking*)

BRIAN   . . . people don't want to let go. Do they?

VOICE OF INTERVIEWER   How do you mean, Brian?

BRIAN   They think it's a mistake, they think it's supposed to last forever. I'll never understand that. My God, it's the one thing in this world you can be sure of! No matter who are you, no matter what you do, no matter anything—sooner or later—it's going to happen. You're going to die.

> (BRIAN *is a graceful man . . . simple, direct, straightforward. He possesses an agile mind and a childlike joy about life.*)

. . . and that's a relief—if you think about it. I should say if you think clearly about it.

VOICE OF INTERVIEWER   I'm not sure I follow you.

BRIAN   Well, the trouble is that most of us spend our entire lives trying to *forget* that we're going to die. And some of us even succeed. It's like pulling the cart with*out* the horse. Or is that a poor analogy?

VOICE OF INTERVIEWER   No, Brian. I think it's fine.

BRIAN   Well, you get the gist of it anyway. I'm afraid I've really lost my touch with words. They don't add up as neatly as they used to.

VOICE OF INTERVIEWER   But you're still writing.

BRIAN   Oh, yes. With great abandon. I may have lost touch with the words, but I still have faith in them. Eventually they have to mean *some*thing . . . give or take a few thousand monkeys, a few thousand typewriters. I'm not particular. Am I being helpful or just boring?

VOICE OF INTERVIEWER   Very helpful.

BRIAN Well, I don't see how. Too much thinking and talking. My former wife once said to me, "We've done enough thinking. Couldn't we just dance for a few years?" (*He laughs.*)

VOICE OF INTERVIEWER Did you?

BRIAN No. I have lousy feet. Instead, I started going on about music and mathematics, the difference between Apollonian airs and Dionysian rites, explaining to her the history of dance and the struggle with form . . . and before I finished the first paragraph, she was gone . . .

> (*The lights fade on the porch area of the cottage where* JOE *and* MAGGIE *are. Then they start to come up on the living room area of the cottage.* BRIAN *continues his interview*)

VOICE OF INTERVIEWER Gone for good?

BRIAN Like a bat out of hell.

VOICE OF INTERVIEWER I see.

BRIAN So do I . . . now. But then I didn't. I became totally irrational . . . idiotic, in the Greek sense of the word. I blamed her, I damned her, I hated her . . . I missed her. I got so worked up I began to realize what she was talking about. You see, I'd lost the energy of it, the magic of it. No wonder she left. After all, the universe isn't a syllogism, it's a miracle. Isn't it? And if you can believe in one small part of it, then you can believe in all of it. And if you can believe in all of it . . . well, that *is* a reason for dancing, isn't it?

VOICE OF INTERVIEWER What happened to her?

BRIAN Beverly? Oh, she's still dancing as far as I know.

VOICE OF INTERVIEWER I see.

BRIAN Well, every life makes sense on its own terms, I suppose. She must be very happy. I'm sure of that. Otherwise she would have come back. There I go, rambling on again. I'm sorry.

VOICE OF INTERVIEWER   You seem to have everything so well thought out.

(*In the living room area of the cottage,* MARK *enters. He is a young man, passionately intelligent, sexually attractive.*)

BRIAN (*Still talking to the* INTERVIEWER)   Well, I think it's important to be sensible. Even about the miraculous. Otherwise you lose track of what it's all about.

VOICE OF INTERVIEWER   How is Mark?

BRIAN (*Smiles*)   Speaking of the miraculous . . . ? Well, he's fine.

MARK (*In the living room, looking around*)   Brian?

BRIAN (*To* INTERVIEWER)   What's the official line on him now?

VOICE OF INTERVIEWER   How do you mean?

BRIAN   Well, I know these are supposed to be strictly family situations. I'm curious. I mean, what are we calling him this week? Nephew? Cousin? Butler?

VOICE OF INTERVIEWER   No. I have him down as a friend.

BRIAN   I see.

VOICE OF INTERVIEWER   In the Greek sense of the word.

BRIAN (*Laughs*)   Very good. Very good.

VOICE OF INTERVIEWER   He's welcome to come and talk to us if he likes.

(*In the living room area,* MARK *takes off his jacket, throws it on a chair, sits down and takes out a package . . .*)

BRIAN   Well, we've talked a lot about it already. Generally, we have the same opinion on the subject. Wisdom doesn't always come with age. Occasionally the young can be as rational as you or I.

(MARK *carefully takes six or seven bottles of medication from the package. He makes notes of each label, copying down the information in a small pad.)*

VOICE OF INTERVIEWER Yes. I suppose they can.

BRIAN (*Checking his watch*) My watch is stopped. How long have I been babbling?

VOICE OF INTERVIEWER It doesn't matter. There's no hurry.

BRIAN Not for you, maybe. Some of us are on a tighter schedule.

VOICE OF INTERVIEWER I am sorry. I didn't mean . . .

BRIAN (*Laughs*) It's all right. It's all right. You mustn't take all of this too seriously. I don't . . . Our dreams are beautiful, our fate is sad. But day by day, it's generally pretty funny.

We can talk again tomorrow, if you want. I don't mind. It's a bit of a shock, that's all. You always think . . . no matter what they tell you . . . you always think you have more time. And you don't.

But I appreciate what you're trying to do here, and I do enjoy being a guinea pig.

VOICE OF INTERVIEWER Good. Very good.

BRIAN Tomorrow, then. If I'm still breathing. Or even if I'm not, I don't think it'll stop me from talking.

VOICE OF INTERVIEWER Yes. Tomorrow.

(The lights fade on the Interview Area and come up on the living room. MARK *puts the medicine in a bookcase that is already loaded with bottles of pills and boxes of medical supplies.*

BEVERLY *comes bursting into the living room, blowing a party horn.)*

BEVERLY Surprise! Oh, who are you? I'm sorry. I'm looking for Brian . . . uh . . . Two. They said cottage two. I must have . . .

MARK No, you didn't . . .

BEVERLY I didn't?

MARK No. This is two. This is cottage two.

BEVERLY Oh.

MARK Yes.

BEVERLY Thank ~~God~~. *(Pause)* Is . . . uh . . .

MARK *(A little uncomfortable)* No. Not at the moment. But he should be back any minute.

BEVERLY Good.

> *(Another pause. They look at each other.)*

I wanted to surprise him and he's not here. Well . . . surprise!

> *(BEVERLY starts to walk around the cottage. She is an extremely attractive woman. Middle-aged. She's dressed curiously in what was once a very expensive, chic evening dress. But it is now soiled and torn. She also has over and around the dress about twenty odd pieces of jewelry attached wherever there is room for them. In her hand a noisemaker that squeaks uncheerfully, and over everything, a yellow slicker raincoat and rubber boots. Looking around)*

BEVERLY Hmn. Very nice. Very nice.

MARK Glad you like it.

BEVERLY All the comforts of home. Amazing what you can do with a coffin if you put your mind to it.

MARK What?!!

BEVERLY Oh, sorry. Sorry. Introductions first. That way you'll know who you're throwing out. *(She extends her hand in a handshake.)* I'm Beverly. No doubt you've . . .

MARK Yes.

BEVERLY That's what I figured.

MARK Brian's wife.

BEVERLY Ex-wife.

MARK Former.

BEVERLY Yes. Former. Former wife. He prefers former, doesn't he?

MARK (*Shakes her hand*) Yes. I figured it was you.

BEVERLY You did?

MARK Yes . . . it wasn't hard.

BEVERLY No, I guess not. (*She smiles*) And you're
. . . uh . . .

MARK Yes.

BEVERLY Yes. I figured.

MARK Mark.

BEVERLY Great. Well.

MARK Well. (*Pause*)

BEVERLY Well, now that we know who we are . . .
how about a drink.

MARK A what?

BEVERLY A drink. A drink.

MARK Oh, no.

BEVERLY No?

MARK No. We don't keep any liquor here. I could get
you some coffee or some penicillin, if you'd like.

BEVERLY No. No. *I* was inviting *you.*
  (*Out of her tote bag she pulls a half finished bottle of Scotch.*)
I had an accident with the Scotch on the way out
here. There's quite a dent in it. (*She laughs.* MARK
doesn't.) Anyway, we both look like we could use a
little. Hmn?

MARK No. I don't drink.

BEVERLY (*Rummaging in her bag*) Ah, a dope man.

MARK Neither. I like to avoid as much poison as possible.

BEVERLY I see.

MARK   Anyway, it's really not the time or place, is it?

BEVERLY   Oh, I don't know.

MARK   Well, you go ahead. If you feel you have to.

BEVERLY   No. No, really. I don't *need* it. I mean, I'm not . . . forget it.

> (*She looks remorsefully at the bottle, takes off the cap, takes a swig, replaces the cap and puts the bottle back in the tote bag.*
>
> MARK *stares at her, obviously displeased by the action. There is a pause.* BEVERLY *smiles.* MARK *does not.*)

So. How is he?

MARK   Dying. How are you?

BEVERLY   (*Taken aback*) Oooops. Let's start again. Is he feeling any pain?

MARK   Are you?

BEVERLY   Strike two. Well, I think we've got it all straight now. He's dying. I'm drunk. And you're ~~mad~~. Did I leave anything out?

MARK   No, I think that just about covers it.

BEVERLY   Tell me. How is he?

MARK   Hard to say. One day he's flat on his ass, the next day he's running around like a two year old. But he is terminal—officially. They moved him down to these cottages because there's nothing they can do for him in the hospital. But he can't go home, either.

There's some pain. But it's tolerable. At least he makes it seem tolerable. They keep shooting him full of cortisone.

BEVERLY   Ouch!

MARK   Yes. Ouch. You should be prepared, I guess.

BEVERLY   Prepared for what?

MARK   The cortisone.

BEVERLY Why? They don't give it to the visitors, do they?

MARK No. I mean it has side effects. It . . . well, you may not notice it, but the skin goes sort of white and puffy. It changed the shape of his face for a while, and he started to get really fat.

BEVERLY His whole body?

MARK Yes. His whole body.

BEVERLY Charming.

MARK Well, don't get too upset. A lot of it's been corrected, but he's still very pale. And he has fainting spells. They're harmless. Well, that's what they tell me. But it's embarrassing for him because he falls down a lot and his face gets a little purple for a minute.

BEVERLY All the details. You're very graphic.

MARK It happens a lot. The details aren't easy to forget.

BEVERLY I guess not.

MARK I just want you to know. If you're staying around. I mean, I think it would hurt him if people noticed.

BEVERLY Well, if he turns purple and falls on the floor, it'd be sort of difficult not to notice, wouldn't it?

MARK (*Taken aback*) What?

BEVERLY I mean, what do people *usually* do when it happens?

MARK I don't know. I mean, there hasn't been anyone here except me and . . .

BEVERLY And you have everything pretty much under control.

MARK I do my best.

BEVERLY I'm sure you do.

MARK   Look. I don't mean to be rude or stupid about
this . . .

BEVERLY   Why not? I like people to be rude and stupid.
It's one of the ways you can be sure they're still alive.
Oh dear, I did it again, didn't I?

MARK   Yes. You have to understand—I mean, you will
be careful, won't you?

BEVERLY   About what?

MARK   That's exactly what I mean. You're . . . I'm
sorry, but you're very stoned, aren't you? And you're
dressed in funny clothes, and you're saying a lot of
funny things but I'm just not sure, frankly, what the
~~fuck~~ you're doing here.

BEVERLY   (*Still flip*) Neither am I. You sure you
wouldn't like a drink?

MARK   Positive. Look, please, don't you think it'd be
better if you came back some other time, like tomorrow or next year or something?

BEVERLY   I'd just have to get drunk all over again.

MARK   I mean, it's sort of a delicate situation, right
now. He's had a very bad time of it and any kind of,
well, disturbance . . .

BEVERLY   Such as me? Oh, you'll get used to it. You
just have to think of me as your average tramp.

MARK   . . . any disturbance might be dangerous, especially psychologically and . . . ~~Shit!~~ I sound like an
idiot, the way I'm talking. But you don't seem to be
understanding ~~a goddamn~~ word I'm saying!

BEVERLY   No. I am. I am. You know, you don't *look*
~~like a faggot.~~

MARK   Oh, for Christ's sake!

BEVERLY   No, I mean it . . . I mean, I didn't expect . . .

MARK Well, you'll get used to it. You just have to
think of me as your average cocksucker. All right?

BEVERLY Good. Now we're getting someplace. Are
you sure you wouldn't like a drink?

MARK *No!* I would not like a drink. *You* have a drink.
Have two. Take off your clothes. Make yourself at
home. (*He grabs his jacket and heads for the door.*)
When you're ready to throw up, the bathroom is in
there. (*He exits.*)

BEVERLY (*Left with the bottle*) Hey!
(*The lights come up on the porch area where*
STEVE *is just coming out of the cottage to join*
MAGGIE *and* JOE.)

STEVE Hey! Is this place bugged or what?

JOE Bugged?

MAGGIE (*Reaching into a shopping bag*) I brought
some Lysol. Here.

STEVE No. Bugged. *Wired.* What do they do? Listen
in with hidden cameras?

JOE (*Laughing*) Yeah. Every move. Every word.

MAGGIE Joe, cut it out.
(*Meanwhile, as this scene continues,* AGNES
wheels FELICITY *on stage and to the kitchen area.*
AGNES *sings softly as she is pushing the wheelchair.*)

AGNES Holy God, we praise thy name.

STEVE (*Continuing*) But they got wires near the bed.

JOE That's for me. Don't worry about it.

MAGGIE (*Changing the subject*) Here. (*To* STEVE)
You take this stuff inside. And keep the noise down.

JOE (*To* MAGGIE) Come on in, Maggie, I'll show you
around.

MAGGIE No. I want to stay outside. For a while, it's
nice.

STEVE (*Runs back into the cottage*)   I'll get my guitar . . .

JOE   You like it, don't you?

MAGGIE   Sure. It's nice. (*Calling*) Stephen, you help me with this . . .

JOE (*Overlapping*)   I knew you would. I'll take you for a walk later. They got a swimming pool. And a tennis court. There's a little river, just a little one, runs back through the trees. Over there. I'll show you later. We got time. There's no hurry.

MAGGIE   Stephen!

JOE   Ah, leave him be. I'll get this. (*He starts to pick up the bags.*)

MAGGIE   No, you rest. Stephen!

JOE   I can get it. The more exercise I get, the better I feel.

MAGGIE (*Stopping him*)   There's no sense pushing it, huh? Steve can do it.

(STEVE *comes out of the cottage with his guitar. He sits down and starts to play it.*)

MAGGIE   Put that thing down and give your father a hand.

JOE (*To* STEVE)   Wait till you see, dad. From the north side, near the gate when you come in, you can see the whole valley. All squared off and patched up with farms like a quilt. Hundreds of them. I'll show you.

STEVE   Farms? They got farms?

JOE   Yeah. Hundreds of them.

MAGGIE   Stephen, take this bag inside. Put this one in the kitchen. (*To* JOE) You got a kitchen?

JOE   Sure. A kitchen, a bathroom, two bedrooms, a living room . . .

STEVE (*Overlapping*)   We never did get our farm. We should do that. We should get that farm. (*He takes bag inside*)

JOE   Well, maybe we should have. A little place . . .

MAGGIE   (*To* STEVE)   There's more here, when you're finished, so hurry up.

JOE   A little place like this . . .

MAGGIE   Don't start on the farm, for God's sake. It always ends up bad when you start on the farm.

STEVE   (*Returning*)   We could sit out every night, singing and howling at the moon. (*He howls like a wolf.*)

MAGGIE   (*Getting more and more agitated*)   Stephen, be quiet. Where do you think you are? This goes in the bedroom.

STEVE   Aren't you ever coming in?

MAGGIE   (*A little too firmly*)   I'll go in when I'm good and ready.

(STEVE *exits with suitcase*)

JOE   (*Noticing* MAGGIE's *nervousness, trying to keep things happy.*)   It might have worked, Maggie. See me all dressed up in coveralls. Early morning, up with the sun. What do you think?

MAGGIE   What do you know about running a farm?

JOE   Nothing. What do *you* know?

MAGGIE   Nothing. (*More irritated*)   It's a lot of work. I don't want to hear about it.

JOE   A little hard work'll never kill you.

MAGGIE   Don't tell me about hard work.

JOE   It's good for you.

MAGGIE   Good for *you*. Not for me. Milk the cows, clean the chicken coop, who would have done that, huh?

STEVE   (*Returning*)   We could have had a couple hundred acres . . .

JOE   No, someplace small, something we could keep our hands on. Al and Lena had that place, we used to go every Sunday.

MAGGIE It was dirty.

STEVE No, it wasn't.

MAGGIE And I never had anything to say to them, anyway. Out there in the sticks. Who do you see out there? Chickens and pigs.

JOE They had neighbors.

MAGGIE Chickens and pigs.

JOE You get used to all that . . .

MAGGIE I don't want to hear about it. Here, Stephen. It's the last one. Put it anywhere.

STEVE (*To* MAGGIE) You would too have liked it. Get a little chicken shit between your toes, kiss a few pigs . . . It'd change your whole disposition . . .
>   (*He grabs the bag and* MAGGIE *and starts whirling her around*)

MAGGIE (*Almost laughing*) Cut it out! Stephen!

STEVE (*Starts to tickle her and push her toward the cottage*) Come on inside, Chicken Lady. I'll show you the roost!
>   (MAGGIE *is laughing hard now.* STEVE *clucks like a chicken, tickling her, and steering her toward the cottage.* JOE *laughs and joins them.*)

JOE Come on, Maggie. We got you.
>   (*He grabs her hand and pulls her toward the cottage.*)

MAGGIE (*Laughing hysterically*) Joe . . . ! No . . . I don't . . . !

STEVE Chickens and pigs! Chickens and pigs!

JOE Come on inside, Maggie. Come on!

MAGGIE No . . . I don't . . . want to go inside . . . No . . . ! Joe!
>   (*Suddenly* MAGGIE *turns and slaps* STEVE *hard across the face. She is terrified.*)
I'm not going in there! Now stop it!

(*Nobody moves for a moment.* STEVE *is stunned.*
MAGGIE *turns away from them.* JOE *goes to* STEVE
and puts his arm around him.)

STEVE I'm going inside to practice . . .

JOE Sure. (*He musses* STEVE's *hair and kisses him on
the cheek.*)

STEVE (*Picks up his guitar and goes to the cottage door.
Then he turns, looks at* MAGGIE. *Then he says to* JOE
. . .) There's a . . . there's a whole lot of shit I got
to tell you. We can talk, huh? Not to worry you, but
just so you know . . . There's a whole lot . . . well,
we can talk, huh?

JOE Sure, dad.
(STEVE *goes inside.* JOE *looks at* MAGGIE, *not
knowing what came over her.*)
Maggie?

MAGGIE I didn't tell him.

JOE What?

MAGGIE (*Still turned away from him*) I didn't tell him.
Stephen. I didn't . . .

JOE Oh, no. No, Maggie. What's the matter with you?

MAGGIE I couldn't.

JOE He doesn't know?
(MAGGIE *shakes her head "No."*)
What does he think? He thinks I'm going home with
you? Maggie? Why didn't you tell him?

MAGGIE I couldn't.

JOE Why not?

MAGGIE Because . . . it isn't true. It isn't true. It
isn't . . .
(*She runs off away from the cottage.* JOE *is
stunned. He sits down on the porch steps and
puts his head in his hands.
The lights come up on the Interview Area.*
AGNES *is pushing* FELICITY *to the area.* FELICITY *is*

wide awake now. She is about sixty or seventy years old. She is singing vaguely to herself. The INTERVIEWER *is with her, trying to get her attention.*)

INTERVIEWER . . . but you don't have to talk to us if you don't want to. Felicity?

(*She continues to sing to herself.*)

If you'd rather not talk now, we can wait until tomorrow.

(*She pays no attention to him.*)

Shall we do that? Shall we wait until tomorrow?

(*No response.*)

Felicity?

(*No response.*)

Well, why don't we do that, then? Why don't we wait, and later if you feel . . .

FELICITY ~~Piss~~ poor.

INTERVIEWER What?

FELICITY Your attitude. It's a ~~piss~~ poor way to treat people.

INTERVIEWER But, Felicity . . .

(AGNES *returns to the kitchen area of the cottage.*)

FELICITY But, but, but!

INTERVIEWER Please . . .

FELICITY Please what?! All right. All right. You want to talk? Let's talk. "I feel fine." Is that what you want to hear? Of course it is. I feel fine, there's no pain, I'm as blind as I was yesterday, my bowels are working—and that's all I got to say about it.

INTERVIEWER We're only trying to help.

FELICITY Well I don't need any more help from you. Do I?

INTERVIEWER Well, we don't know.

FELICITY Of course you know. I've just told you. I've just said it, haven't I?

INTERVIEWER Yes.

FELICITY Well, then . . . there you are. You should learn to listen.

INTERVIEWER Yes.

FELICITY What, have you got your friends out there again? All come to look at the dead people.

INTERVIEWER Felicity . . .

FELICITY He doesn't like me to say things like that. He's sensitive. Why don't you go hide yourself out there with the rest of them?

INTERVIEWER Would you like me to . . . ?

FELICITY No. (*Beat*) No. You stay where you are.

INTERVIEWER All right.

FELICITY How do I look today?

INTERVIEWER You look fine.

FELICITY You're a liar. I look like I feel. I smell, too. (*She turns away from him*)

INTERVIEWER Are you tired, Felicity?

FELICITY No.

INTERVIEWER Do you want to talk some more today?

FELICITY No.

INTERVIEWER All right then. Do you want to go back to the cottage?

FELICITY No.

INTERVIEWER Will you tell us if you're in pain?

FELICITY No.

INTERVIEWER You could help us if you talked to us.

FELICITY Help you? Help you? Which one of us is kicking the bucket? Me? Me or you?

INTERVIEWER Well . . .

FELICITY   Come on. Spit it out. Don't be shy. You're not stupid on top of everything else, are you? One of us is dying and it isn't you, is it?

INTERVIEWER   No. You are the patient.

FELICITY   Patient?! Patient, hell! I'm the corpse. I have one lung, one plastic bag for a stomach, and two springs and a battery where my heart used to be. You cut me up and took everything that wasn't nailed down. Sons of bitches.

INTERVIEWER   But we're not your doctors, Mrs. Thomas. We have nothing to do with . . .

FELICITY   (*Overlapping*)   We're not your doctors . . . Claire . . .

INTERVIEWER   What?

FELICITY   Claire . . .

INTERVIEWER   Mrs. Thomas? Are you all right?

FELICITY   I'm all right! I'm all right! I'll tell you when I'm not all right. It isn't five, is it? Is it five yet?

INTERVIEWER   Five?

FELICITY   Sons of bitches . . . my daughter, Claire.

INTERVIEWER   Yes.

FELICITY   She writes to me regularly. A letter almost every day. I have them at the cottage.

INTERVIEWER   That's very nice!

FELICITY   Yes!

INTERVIEWER   Where does she live?

FELICITY   Who?

INTERVIEWER   Your daughter, Claire.

FELICITY   Yes. I've kept them all—every letter she ever sent me.

INTERVIEWER   That's a good idea.

FELICITY   So I'll have them when I go home. She's a good girl, my Claire.

INTERVIEWER Where is she now?

FELICITY Now?

INTERVIEWER Yes.

FELICITY She's with me.

INTERVIEWER Where?

FELICITY Here. At the house.

INTERVIEWER The house?

FELICITY Yes. You don't run a place like this on dreams. It takes hard work. The property isn't much but the stock is good. We showed a profit in '63. Nobody was more surprised than I was—but we did it. How do I look today?

INTERVIEWER You look fine. Do you want to talk about Claire?

FELICITY I look terrible.

INTERVIEWER The more we know, the easier it is for us to understand how you feel.

FELICITY No. Claire isn't with me anymore. She'll be here soon. But she isn't here now. Agnes is with me now . . . (*She calls out*) Agnes! (*To the* INTERVIEWER) Agnes is my oldest.

INTERVIEWER Yes, we . . .

FELICITY (*Calling again*) Agnes!!!

(*The lights come up on the cottage behind* FELICITY. AGNES *is discovered inside, writing at a table. When she hears her mother's voice, she gets up slowly, folds the paper she has been writing on, puts it into an envelope, seals the envelope and puts it into her pocket.*

AGNES *is a middle-aged woman—very neat, very tense, very tired. She has tried all her life to do the right thing, and the attempt has left her confused, awkward, and unsure of herself.*

When she hears her mother call, she goes to her.)

FELICITY Agnes!

INTERVIEWER Mrs. Thomas . . . ?

FELICITY (*Her voice and manner growing harder again*) Claire has two children now, two beautiful, twin angels . . . (*Calling*) Agnes! (*To* INTERVIEWER) Agnes has me.

AGNES (*Approaching the Interview Area*) Yes, Mama. I'm coming.

FELICITY She's a little slow. It's not her fault. She takes after her father. Not too pretty and not too bright. Is she here yet?

AGNES (*Standing behind* FELICITY'S *wheelchair*) Yes, Mama. I'm here.

FELICITY (*To* INTERVIEWER) There. You see what I mean? You be careful of Agnes. She's jealous.

AGNES (*A little embarrassed*) Mama . . . please.

FELICITY Get me out of here.

AGNES (*To* INTERVIEWER) Is that all for today?

INTERVIEWER Yes, thank you, Agnes, that's . . .

FELICITY (*Overlapping*) That's all. That's all! Now take me back.

AGNES Yes, Mama.
    (*She turns the wheelchair and starts to push it toward the cottage.*)

FELICITY Easy! Easy! You'll upset my internal wire works.

AGNES I'm sorry. (*Turning back to the* INTERVIEWER) Same time tomorrow?

INTERVIEWER Yes. And if you have time, Agnes, we'd like to talk to you.

AGNES Me?

FELICITY We'll see about tomorrow. ~~You sons of bitches.~~

AGNES (*To* INTERVIEWER) All right.

FELICITY   Push, Agnes. Push!

AGNES   Yes, Mama. Off we go.
   (*They go up to the kitchen area of the cottage.*)

FELICITY   That's the spirit. Put some balls into it!
   (*Back in the cottage,* BRIAN *enters the living
   room area where* BEVERLY *is waiting.*)

BEVERLY   Caro! Caro! You old fart! Vieni qua!

BRIAN (*Delighted*)   Sweet Jesus! Beverly!

BEVERLY   My God, he even remembers my name!
   What a mind! (*She hugs and kisses him.*)

BRIAN   What a picture!

BEVERLY (*Taking off her coat to show her dress and
   jewels*)   All my medals. All of them! I wore as many
   of them as I could fit.

BRIAN   Fantastic.

BEVERLY   Everything I could carry. I tried to get
   X-rays done but there wasn't time. Inside and out. I'll
   strip later and show you all of it.

BRIAN (*Laughing*)   Good. Good. What a surprise!
   (*Another embrace*) I'm so happy you've come.
   Where's Mark? Have you met him?

BEVERLY   Oh, yes. He's beautiful. A little cool, but I'm
   sure there's a heart in there somewhere.

BRIAN   Where is he?

BEVERLY   Well . . . he's gone.

BRIAN   What?

BEVERLY   It's my fault. I made a very sloppy entrance. I
   think he left in lieu of punching me in the mouth.

BRIAN   I don't believe it.

BEVERLY   It's true. But I do like him.

BRIAN   Good. So do I.

BEVERLY (*Insinuating*)   So I gather.

BRIAN (*Cheerfully*)   Uh-uh. Careful.

BEVERLY   Is he any good?

BRIAN   Beverly!

BEVERLY   Well, what's it like?

BRIAN   "It?"

BEVERLY   Yes. Him, you, it . . . you know I'm a glutton for pornography. Tell me, quick.

BRIAN *(Laughs)*   Oh, no.

BEVERLY   No?

BRIAN   No. And that's final. I refuse to discuss it.

BEVERLY   Brian, that's not fair. Here I am all damp in my panties and you're changing the subject. Now come on. Tell me all about it.

BRIAN   Absolutely not. I'm much too happy.

BEVERLY   Brian . . . I was married to you, I deserve an explanation. Isn't that what I'm supposed to say?

BRIAN   Yes, but you're too late. No excuses, no explanations. *(Singing)* He is my sunshine, my only sunshine . . . He's the—pardon the expression—cream in my coffee—the milk in my tea—He will always be my necessity . . .

BEVERLY   Ah, but is he enough?

BRIAN   More than enough.

BEVERLY   Shucks.

BRIAN *(Laughs)*   Sorry, but it's out of my hands. All of it. Some supreme logic has taken hold of my life. And in the absence of any refutable tomorrow, every insane thing I do today seems to make a great deal of sense.

BEVERLY   What the hell does that mean?

BRIAN   It means there are more important things in this world.

BEVERLY   More important than what?

BRIAN   More important than worrying about who is fucking whom.

BEVERLY   You *are* happy, aren't you?

BRIAN   Ecstatic. I'm even writing again.

BEVERLY   Oh, my God. You couldn't be *that* happy!

BRIAN   Why not?

BEVERLY   Brian, you're a terrible writer, and you know it.

BRIAN   So?

BEVERLY   Outside of that wonderful book of crossword puzzles, your greatest contribution to the literary world was your retirement.

BRIAN   (*Finishes the sentence with her*) . . . was my retirement. Yes. Well, the literary world, such as it is, will have to brave the storm. Because I'm back.

BEVERLY   But why?

BRIAN   Pure and unadulterated masochism. No. It's just that when they told me I was on the way out . . . so to speak . . . I realized that there was a lot to do that I hadn't done yet. So I figured I better get off my ass and start working.

BEVERLY   Doing what?

BRIAN   Everything! Everything! It's amazing what you can accomplish. Two rotten novels, twenty-seven boring short stories, several volumes of tortured verse including twelve Italian sonnets and one epic investigation of the Firth of Forth Bridge . . .

BEVERLY   The what?

BRIAN   The bridge. The railroad bridge in Scotland. The one Hitchcock used in *The Thirty-nine Steps*. You remember. We saw the picture on our honeymoon.

BEVERLY   Oh, yes.

BRIAN   And I swore that one day I would do a poem about it. Well, I've done it.

BEVERLY   Thank Heavens!

BRIAN Yes. Four hundred stanzas—trochaic hexameters with rhymed couplets. (*He demonstrates the rhythm*) *Da*-da-da, *Da*-da-da, *Da*-da-da, *Da*-da-da, *Da*-da-da, *Da*-da-da, *Da*-da-da-*Dee!* It's perfectly ghastly. But it's done. I've also completed nearly one hundred and thirty-six epitaphs, the largest contribution to the Forest Lawn catalogue since Edna St. Vincent Millay, and four autobiographies.

BEVERLY Four?!

BRIAN Yes. Each one under a different name. There's a huge market for dying people right now. My agent assured me.

BEVERLY I don't believe it.

BRIAN It's true. And then we thought we'd give them each one of those insipid dirty titles—like *Sex . . . And the Dying Man!*

BEVERLY Or *The Sensuous Corpse.*

BRIAN Very good.

BEVERLY (*Affectionately*) You idiot. What else?

BRIAN Not too much. For a while they were giving me this drug and my vision was doubled. I couldn't really see to write. So I started to paint.

BEVERLY Paint?

BRIAN Pictures. I did fourteen of them. Really extraordinary stuff. I was amazed. I mean, you know I can't draw a straight line. But with my vision all cockeyed —I could do a bowl of fruit that sent people screaming from the room.

BEVERLY I can believe it. So now you're painting.

BRIAN No, no. They changed the medication again and now all the fruit just looks like fruit again. But I did learn to drive.

BEVERLY A car?

BRIAN Yes.

BEVERLY   Good grief.

BRIAN   Not very well, but with a certain style and
sufficient accuracy to keep myself alive—although that
is beside the point, isn't it? Let's see, what else? I've
become a master at chess, bridge, poker and mah-
jongg, I finally bought a television set, I sold the house
and everything that was in it, closed all bank ac-
counts, got rid of all stocks, bonds, securities, everything.

BEVERLY   What did you do with the money?

BRIAN   I put it in a sock and buried it on Staten Island.

BEVERLY   You did, didn't you?

BRIAN   Almost. I gave back my American Express card,
my BankAmericard—severed all my patriotic connec-
tions. I even closed my account at Bloomingdale's.

BEVERLY   This is serious.

BRIAN   You're damn right it is. I sleep only three hours
a day, I never miss a dawn or a sunset, I say and do
everything that comes into my head. I even sent letters to everyone I know and told them exactly what I
think of them . . . just so none of the wrong people
show up for the funeral. And finally . . . I went to
Passaic, New Jersey.

BEVERLY   For God's sake, why?!

BRIAN   Because I had no desire to go there.

BEVERLY   Then why did you go?

BRIAN   Because I wanted to be absolutely *sure* I had no
desire to go there.

BEVERLY   And now you know.

BRIAN   Yes. I spent two weeks at a Holiday Inn and had
all my meals at Howard Johnson.

BEVERLY   Jesus! You've really gone the limit.

BRIAN   Believe me, Passaic is beyond the limit. Anyway, that's what I've been doing. Every day in every

way, I get smaller and smaller. There's practically
nothing left of me.

BEVERLY   You're disappearing before my very eyes.

BRIAN   Good. You see, the only way to beat this thing
is to leave absolutely nothing behind. I don't want to
leave anything unsaid, undone . . . not a word, not
even a lonely, obscure, silly, worthless thought. I
want it all used up. All of it. That's not too much to
ask, is it?

BEVERLY   No.

BRIAN   That's what I thought. Then I can happily leap
into my coffin and call it a day. Lie down, close my
eyes, shut my mouth and disappear into eternity.

BEVERLY   As easy as that?

BRIAN   Like falling off a log.

> (BRIAN *laughs.* BEVERLY *laughs. And then the
> laughter slowly dies.*
>
> BEVERLY *goes to him, takes his hands, holds
> them for a moment. Long pause.*)

It shows. Doesn't it?

BEVERLY   You're shaking.

BRIAN   I can't help it. I'm scared to death.

BEVERLY   It's a lot to deal with.

BRIAN   No. Not really. It's a little thing. I mean, all this
. . . this is easy. Pain, discomfort . . . that's all part of
living. And I'm just as alive now as I ever was. And I
will be alive right up to the last moment. *That's* the
hard part, that last fraction of a second—when you
know that the next fraction of a second—I can't seem
to fit that moment into my life . . . You're absolutely
alone facing an absolute unknown and there is absolutely nothing you can do about it . . . except give in.

> (*Pause*)

BEVERLY   That's how I felt the first time I lost my vir-
ginity.

BRIAN (*Smiles*) How was it the second time?

BEVERLY Much easier.

BRIAN There. You see? The real trouble with dying is you only get to do it once. (BRIAN *drifts into the thought.*)

BEVERLY (*Pulling him back*) I brought you some champagne.

BRIAN I'm sorry. I must be the most tedious person alive.

BEVERLY As a matter of fact, you are. Thank God you won't be around much longer.

BRIAN (*Looking at the champagne*) I hope you don't think I'm going to pass away drunk. I intend to be cold sober.

BEVERLY No. No. I thought we could break it on your ass and shove you off with a great bon voyage, confetti and streamers all over the grave.

BRIAN (*Laughing*) Perfect. Perfect. I've missed your foolishness.

BEVERLY You hated my foolishness.

BRIAN I never understood it.

BEVERLY Neither did I. But it was the only way. The only way I knew.

BRIAN Well, all those roads, they all go to Rome, as they say.

BEVERLY Yes. But why is it I always seem to end up in Naples?

(BRIAN AND BEVERLY *embrace.*

The lights come up on the kitchen area of the cottage where AGNES *is singing quietly.*)

AGNES (*Singing*)
Holy God, we praise thy name
Lord of all, we bow before Thee
All on earth thy scepter claim
All in heaven above adore thee.

FELICITY (*Who appeared to be asleep*)   What the hell is that?

AGNES   It's a hymn, Mama.

FELICITY   Hymn! The time for hymns is when I'm in the coffin. Sing us a song!

AGNES   A song?

FELICITY   You know what a song *is*, don't you?

AGNES   Of course I know what a song is, but I don't think I know anything . . .

FELICITY (*Singing*)   "Roll me over, in the clover, Lay me down, roll me over, do it again . . ."

AGNES   Mama, people can hear you.

FELICITY   Do them good.
"This is number one and the fun is just begun
Lay me down, roll me over, do it again . . ."

AGNES   All right, Mama. I'll get you some tea.

FELICITY (*Ignoring her*)
"Roll me over, in the clover
Lay me down, roll me over, do it again . . ."

AGNES   Would you like that? Would you like some tea, Mama?

FELICITY   Put me by the table.

FELICITY (*More singing*)   AGNES   You should try to
"This is number two   rest, Mama. This medi-
and his hand is on my   cine does no good if
shoe.   you   exhaust   your-
Lay me down, roll me   self . . .
over, do it again . . ."
        (AGNES *wheels her to the table*)

FELICITY   Other side! Other side!
        (AGNES *moves her to the other side of the table*)

FELICITY   "This is num-   AGNES   We've   done
ber three and his hand   enough singing, now,
is on my knee.   Mama. I want you to

Lay me down, roll me   stop. Please.
over . . ."

    (FELICITY *feels for the edge of the table.*)

FELICITY Closer! Closer!

AGNES (*Pushing her closer to the table*) There. Is that all right?

FELICITY (*Ignoring her*) "This is number four and . . ." I don't remember four. What's four?

AGNES (*Setting up a game of checkers*) I don't know, Mama. I don't think I know this song.

FELICITY "This is number five and his hand is on my thigh . . ." Do you know that one?

AGNES No, Mama. I don't. *Very tired.*

FELICITY They'll pass you by, Agnes. They will.

AGNES Who, Mama?

FELICITY They'll leave you at the station with your suitcase in your hand and a big gardenia tacked onto your collar. Sons of bitches.

AGNES I'm not anxious to be going anywhere.

FELICITY "This is number six and his hands are on my tits . . ."

AGNES Mama!

FELICITY Does *that* make you anxious?

AGNES No.

FELICITY Well, it makes *me* anxious. And I haven't even *got* tits anymore.

AGNES I'll get you some tea, Mama.

FELICITY Tea . . . tea . . . tea . . . !

AGNES Please, Mama. I'm very tired.

FELICITY (*At the top of her lungs*) "This is number seven and we're on our way to heaven . . . !"

AGNES (*Suddenly and violently screams at her*) Mama!!!! *Stop it!!*

(FELICITY *stops singing. She looks hurt, confused. She seems to drift off again as she did earlier, all her energy draining away.*

AGNES *covers her mouth quickly, immediately ashamed and sorry for her outburst.*

There is a long silence. BRIAN *goes to the stage left porch.* JOE *crosses to the downstage porch and sits on the bench.*

FELICITY (*Very gentle, very weak*) Put 'em away. Put 'em away. Shoot 'em and bury them. You can't get good milk from sick cows. Can you?

AGNES No, Mama. You can't.

FELICITY They're not doing anybody any good. Standing around, making noises like it mattered. Bursting their bellies and there's nothing good inside. Just a lot of bad milk. Put 'em away. You see to that machinery.

AGNES Yes, Mama. I will.

FELICITY It wants attention.

AGNES We'll manage. We can sell off some of the land, if we have to.

FELICITY But not the house.

AGNES No, not the house. We'll keep the house.

FELICITY What . . . what time did you say it was?

AGNES Oh . . . about four. Four-fifteen.

FELICITY Claire? Claire . . . ?

AGNES No, Mama. It's Agnes.

FELICITY It hurts . . . hurts now . . .

AGNES I know, Mama . . .

FELICITY Make it stop. Make it stop now . . .

AGNES I'll give you some of the medicine.

FELICITY Yes. With some tea. Could I have it with some tea?

AGNES   Yes, Mama. I think so.

FELICITY   Just one cup. Very weak.

AGNES   Yes, Mama. I'll make it for you. (*She goes to make the tea.*)

FELICITY   (*A sudden small panic*)   Agnes . . . ! ?

AGNE: Here, Mama, here. I'm just going to make the tea.

FELICITY   Yes. All right. (*She panics again*) Agnes!

AGNES   (*Takes a wet cloth and wrings it out*)   Yes, Mama. I'm here. (*She goes to* FELICITY *and wipes her brow with the cloth*) It's all right. I'll get you your tea and then I'll read you your letter.

    (STEVE *starts to play* "Goodnight Irene" *on his guitar.*

       MARK *crosses to the down right Interview area.*)

FELICITY   Where are they now?

AGNES   Let me check the calendar.

MARK   I don't want to talk about it. It doesn't do any good to talk about it. I mean, it's just words. Isn't it? Little mirrors. You keep hanging them up like they mean something. You put labels on them. This one is true. This one is false. This one is broken . . . You can see right through it. Well, it all depends on how you look at it. Doesn't it?

FELICITY   When did they say they were coming?

AGNES   Let's see. Today is the fifth. The fifth of May.

MAGGIE   I called home. I told them we got here all right. I told them . . . I don't know . . . I wanted to talk to Pop. But he was asleep. He takes naps now. He gets up every morning at seven and he goes to church. All his life—since the day he was married—you couldn't get him near a church. Now he's seventy-five and he's there every morning. I asked him why, he said it was between him and God. What does that mean?

FELICITY When did they say they were coming?

AGNES Yes. Mexico. They should be passing right through the center of Mexico today.

FELICITY They're moving awfully slow, don't you think?

AGNES Well, it's difficult for them, I imagine. Trying to get so much organized, a family, a whole family and everything else . . . You can't just drop everything and leave. Especially if you live in a foreign country, as they do . . .

BRIAN I asked one of the doctors. I said, why do I shake like this? He said he didn't know . . . I said, well . . . is it a symptom or is it because of the drugs? He said, no. And I said, well, why then? I don't seem to have any control of it. I'm feeling perfectly all right and then I shake.

And he said, try to think if it's ever happened before . . . that kind of thing. And I couldn't. For a long time. And then I remembered being very young . . . I was—oh—five years old. My father was taking me to Coney Island. And we got separated on the train. And I kept trying to ask for directions but I couldn't talk because I was shaking so badly.

It was because I was frightened. That . . . uh . . . That's why I shake now . . . Isn't it?

FELICITY (In great pain) Agnes . . . !!! Agnes.

AGNES Yes, Mama, here. It's all right.

FELICITY Agnes! Sons of bitches . . .

JOE I get dreams now. Every night. I get dreams so big. I never used to dream. But now, every night so big. Every person I ever knew in my life coming through my room, talking and talking and sometimes singing and dancing. Jumping all around my bed. And I get up to go with them, but I can't. The sheets are too heavy and I can't move to save my life. And they keep talking and calling my name, whispering so loud it hurts my ears . . . "Joe" and "Joe" and laughing and singing and I know every one of them and they pull at my arms and my legs and I still can't move. And I'm laughing and singing, too, inside, where you can't hear it . . . And it hurts so bad, but I can't feel it. And I yell back at them, every person I ever knew, and they don't hear me, either, and then the room gets brighter and brighter. So bright I can't see anything anymore. Nobody. Not even me. It's all gone. All white. All gone.

FELICITY Agnes . . . !!

AGNES Yes, Mama.

FELICITY When did they say they were coming?

AGNES I don't know, Mama. Soon. Soon.

FELICITY As long as we know . . . As long as we know they're coming.

AGNES Well, of course they're coming. You wait and see . . . One afternoon, we'll be sitting here, having tea, and that door will fly open like the gates of heaven and there they'll be . . .
     (*She takes a capsule from a small bottle and adds the medication to the cup of tea.*)
. . . two twin angels and our bright-eyed little girl. You wait and see, Mama. You_wait_ . . .
     (*She takes the cup to* FELICITY *and then notices that she is asleep.*)
Mama? Oh, Mama.

BRIAN (*Going to* BEVERLY) Dance with me, Bev.

BEVERLY My pleasure, sir.

MAGGIE Joe?

JOE   We got to tell him, Maggie. We got to tell him.

AGNES   Rest, Mama . . . rest . . .

MARK   It'll all be over in a minute. It just seems to take forever.

(*The lights fade out.*)

ACT TWO

Hi
David

Evening.
Music is coming from the living room area . . . a recording of "Don't Sit Under the Apple Tree." BEVERLY *is dancing around alone,* BRIAN *is sitting on the sofa watching her.* MARK *is in the kitchen area getting a glass of milk.*

As the lights come up, however, we focus on the porch area where MAGGIE *is seated, staring off at the sunset.* JOE *comes down to her, carrying a cup of coffee.*

JOE It's getting dark, Maggie.

MAGGIE (*Very distant*) It's pretty.

JOE Yeah. (*Pause*) You can't sit out here all night. Huh? (MAGGIE *doesn't answer.*) I brought you some coffee. (MAGGIE *takes it.*)

MAGGIE I'm all right. I'm all right. I just need some time, that's all.

JOE I'll get you a sweater.
　　　(JOE *goes back into the cottage, to the UC room and sits. Our focus shifts now into the living room area. It looks like a small party.* BEVERLY *is carrying on and* BRIAN *is enjoying every minute of it.* MARK *is not.*)

BRIAN Another drink for Beverly and then she can show us her scars.

BEVERLY Medals, medals! Not scars.

BRIAN Well, we won't argue the perspective.

MARK (*Giving her a drink*) I don't understand.

BEVERLY Dancing contests. That's a euphemism for balling. First prize, second prize, third prize . . . sometimes just a citation for style. I like to keep Brian informed.

MARK You lost me.

BEVERLY Look. (*She takes off an earring*) Peter somebody. Diamonds. Really. Very pure, very idealistic, an architect. Form follows function . . . I never understood it. (*She tosses the earring into her tote bag*)

BRIAN (*Toasting with his milk*) To Peter!

BEVERLY (*Drinks*) One among many. (*She takes off a bracelet*) This one's copper. A doctor in Colorado Springs. Said it would cure my arthritis and he'd take care of the rest. He didn't. (*She drops the bracelet on the floor*)

BRIAN (*Toasting again*) Colorado Springs!

BEVERLY (*Drinks*) Anyway, I didn't have arthritis. (*She points to a brooch*) This one, God knows. A family heirloom and would I join the collection. No, thank you. (*Takes off a chain necklace with a tooth on it and swings it in a circle*) Claus. Nowegian shark tooth or something. A thousand and one positions, and each one lasted several hours. I couldn't. (*She drops it*)

BRIAN I should hope not.

BEVERLY But I tried. (*Takes another, very similar to the previous one, but smaller.*) Claus' brother. If at first you don't succeed . . . (*Points at a bracelet*) A Russian in Paris. (*Another bracelet*) A Frenchman in Moscow. (*Taking off an ankle bracelet*) Ah . . . a Tunisian in Newfoundland. Really. We met at an airport and made it between flights under his grass skirt. (*Drops it on the couch and then takes off two tiaras*) Two lovely ladies in Biarritz. No comment, thank you. (*Drops it on the sofa*) Oh . . . yes. The Jean Jacques collection. (*Taking off several other pieces*) Jean Jacques. Jean Jacques. Jean Jacques. Jean Jacques. Jean Jacques. You might say I took him for everything he was worth. You'd be wrong. There was a whole lot more I couldn't get my hands on. (*Toasting*) A big one for Jean Jacques.

BRIAN (*Toasting*) Jean Jacques!

BEVERLY (*A little dizzy*) I'm getting sloppy. I tried. Dear Brian, how I tried. (*To* MARK) You're the scholar. What's the exact declension of incompatibility? I tried, they tried, we tried . . .

MARK That's not a declension. That's a conjugation.

BEVERLY No, it wasn't. Not once. Not a single conjugator in the bunch. Not one real dancer. Not one real jump to the music, flat out, no count, foot stomping crazy-man . . . just a lot of tired "declining" people who really didn't want to do anything but sit the next one out. What else? Oh. Last and least, my favorite dress. A gap here, a stain there, a spilled drink, a catch, a tear . . . spots you can hardly see, that won't come out . . . people I hardly knew.

MARK It looks walked over.

BEVERLY Over and over again. Stitch it up, tie it up, wrap it up . . . it keeps coming back for more. Greedy little bitch. Here's a good one. A very well dressed man on a train. Put his hand here, on my leg kept saying over and over again, "Trust me, trust me," and all the time he was beating off under his coat.

MARK That's pathetic.

BEVERLY Oh, I don't know. I think he liked me. Don't you think so? I mean the car was full of attractive younger women and the bast... chose me.

MARK You must have been his type.

BRIAN Mark!

MARK I'm sorry. It just came out.

BEVERLY That's all right.

MARK It's not all right, it stinks.

BEVERLY Okay. It stinks. Forget it. Here's to all of them. The young, the old, the black, the white, the yellow, the lame, the hale, the feebleminded, the poor, the rich, the small and the well endowed . . . all of them. Here's hoping there's better where *they* came from.

MARK (*Getting his jacket and going towards the door*) I'm going out for a walk.

BEVERLY Oh, no. How are we ever going to get to know each other if you keep leaving the room?

BRIAN Don't go, Mark.

MARK I need some air. (*He starts to go.*)

BEVERLY No. Stay. Come on. Please. (*She gets the champagne bottle.*)

MARK Please what? You don't need me here, you've got a captive audience.

BEVERLY Come on. We'll open the champagne and I'll shut up for a while.

MARK Thanks, but I already told you . . .

BEVERLY (*Forcing off the cork*) It's good stuff. I only *look* cheap. Really. Are you sure you wouldn't like . . .

> (*The cork flies off and* BEVERLY *accidentally spills the contents of the bottle on* MARK)

. . . a drink?

MARK (*Sopping wet*) No. Thank you.

BEVERLY (*Really embarrassed, somewhere between giggling and crying*) Oh, God, I'm sorry. Talk about tedious people. I think I feel an exit coming up.

BRIAN (*Goes to her, comforting*) You look very beautiful, Beverly. I should have noticed when I walked in.

BEVERLY I'm tired and drunk.

BRIAN And beautiful.

BEVERLY (*Clings to him for an instant*) I'll miss you, you fucker.

BRIAN I'll miss you, too.

BEVERLY (*To* MARK) Look what I've done. (*She starts to take the jacket from him.*)

MARK (*Not letting go*) It's all right.

BEVERLY No. It's not. I've ruined it.

MARK All right, you've ruined it.

BEVERLY I'll send you another one.

MARK No, I'll have it cleaned.

BEVERLY It won't come out.

MARK Please!

BRIAN (*Grabbing the jacket and throwing it down*) My God, it's only a jacket. Two sleeves, a collar, a piece of cloth. It was probably made by a machine in East Podunk. Why are we wasting this time?

MARK Brian, take it easy . . .

BRIAN No! Not easy. Not easy at all! At this very moment, twelve million stars are pumping light in and out of a three hundred and sixty degree notion of a limited universe. Not easy! At this very moment, a dozen Long Island oysters are stranded in some laboratory in Chicago, opening and closing to the rhythm of the tide—over a thousand miles away. Not easy! At this very moment, the sun is probably hurtling out of control, defying ninety percent of all organized religion—plummeting toward a massive world collision

that was predicted simultaneously by three equally ar-
chaic cultures who had barely invented the wheel. At
this very moment, some simple peasant in Mexico is
planting seeds in his veins with the blind hope that
flowers will bloom on his body before the frost kills
him! And here we stand, the combined energy of our
three magnificent minds focused irrevocably on this
~~fucking~~ jacket.

(*He picks up the jacket and hands it to* MARK.)

~~My God~~. There are more important things I promise
you.

(MARK *does not respond.* BRIAN *goes to* BEVERLY
and takes her in his arms.)

Come on, my beauty, I'll show you a dancer.

(*They begin to do the Lindy.* BRIAN *turns on the
tape recorder and "Don't Sit Under the Apple
Tree" starts to play.*)

BEVERLY (*Laughing*) Brian! Stop!

(*Suddenly* BRIAN *falters. Breathless, he starts to
fall, catches himself, and then falls.*
BEVERLY *goes to him.*)

Brian?! Are you all . . . ?

BRIAN No! No. It's all right. I'm all right. He walks, he
talks, he falls down, he gets up. Life goes on.

MARK Let me give you a hand.

BRIAN Leave me alone.

(*Carefully he exits to the bedroom.* BEVERLY
looks anxiously at MARK)

BEVERLY Do you think you should . . . ?

MARK No. No.

(MARK *doesn't move. Finally,* BEVERLY *follows*
BRIAN *to the bedroom.* BEVERLY *exits.*

MARK *picks up the bottle, turns off the recorder, sits down and starts drinking from the
bottle.*

At the same time, AGNES *comes down to the stool at DR kitchen area, which becomes her Interview Area)*

AGNES (*Speaking to the* INTERVIEWER) I shouldn't stay too long.

INTERVIEWER (*At DL stool, but still miked*) Yes. We won't keep you.

AGNES You said you wanted to see me. Are there people there?

INTERVIEWER Yes.

AGNES I don't know what I can tell you.

INTERVIEWER Well . . .

AGNES The doctors saw her yesterday. They said they were going to change the medication, and after that, they weren't sure . . . Oh, but they must have told you all this.

INTERVIEWER Yes.

AGNES Oh. What . . . what was it you wanted to know, then?

INTERVIEWER Well, we wanted to know about you.

AGNES (*Almost smiles*) Me? Oh, that's . . . (*Then worried*) Why? I've done everything that . . . just like the nurse tells me. I've been very careful to . . .

INTERVIEWER No. No. It isn't that. You're doing very well with her. Much better than anyone could ask. We know that.

AGNES Then . . . what?

INTERVIEWER Well, we were just wondering how you were?

AGNES (*Relieved*) Oh. I'm fine. Is that what you mean? I'm fine.

INTERVIEWER Yes.

AGNES I'm fine.

INTERVIEWER Good.

AGNES Yes. I'm a little tired. And sometimes a headache
. . . I used to get headaches.

INTERVIEWER Oh?

AGNES Yes. Terrible headaches. Mama always said they
were psychosomatic. She said if I concentrated hard
enough, they would go away.

INTERVIEWER And did they?

AGNES As a matter of fact, they did. Not right away.
But after a while . . .

INTERVIEWER Do you still get them?

AGNES What . . . ?

INTERVIEWER The headaches. Do you still get them?

AGNES I don't know. I used to get them so often. Now
sometimes I don't know I have them—until they go
away. You get used to them and you don't feel any
different until they're gone. And I . . . what was it
you wanted to ask me?

INTERVIEWER Tell us about Claire.

AGNES What?

INTERVIEWER Claire. Felicity has been telling us
that . . .

AGNES Claire.

INTERVIEWER Your sister.

AGNES Oh, Claire . . .

INTERVIEWER Yes.

AGNES Claire is my sister.

INTERVIEWER Yes.

AGNES (*With great reluctance*) We were very close.
Our whole family. Especially after my father died.
We were just children then. Mama worked very hard
to keep us together. We had a dairy farm. It was a
beautiful place. Big, old house . . . 1873. And so

much land. It seemed even bigger then . . . I was so little. We were happy.

And then Claire . . . there was a boy . . . well, she left us . . . just like that. She was a lot like Mama. They would fight and yell and throw things at each other . . . they got along very well.

Claire was so beautiful. I would hide in my room. I got so frightened when they fought, but . . . I don't know . . . suddenly the fight would be over and Mama would throw open her arms and curse the day she bore children and Claire would laugh and then Mama would laugh and hug her close . . . and then all of us, we would laugh . . . I can still hear us . . .

But she left. And we never heard from her. Almost a year. The longest year I can remember. Mama waited and waited, but she never wrote or came back to visit . . . nothing. And then one morning, finally, we received a letter from a man in Louisiana. There was an accident . . . something. And Claire was dead. They said at first they thought she was going to be all right, but she was hemorrhaging and . . . This is very hard to remember.

INTERVIEWER But these letters from Claire.

AGNES Yes. You see, it was after Claire died that Mama started to get sick. All of a sudden, she was "old." And she isn't, you know. But she just seemed to give up. I couldn't bring her out of it. Claire could have. But I couldn't. We lost the farm, the house, everything. One thing led to another.

The letters . . . uh . . . It was after one of the last operations. Mama came home from the hospital and she seemed very happy. She was much stronger than ever. She laughed and joked and made fun of me, just like she used to . . . and then she told me she had written a letter while she was in the hospital . . . to

Claire . . . and she said she was very nice to her and she forgave her for not writing and keeping in touch and she asked her to come home to visit and to bring her children . . . Claire had been dead for a long time then.

I didn't know what to do. I tried to tell her . . . I tried . . . but she wouldn't listen . . .

And, of course, no letter came. No reply. And Mama asked every day for the mail. Every day I had to tell her no, there wasn't any. Every day. I kept hoping she would forget, but she didn't. And when there wasn't any letter for a long time, she started to get worse. She wouldn't talk and when she did she accused me of being jealous and hiding the letters and sometimes . . . I didn't know what to do . . . So . . . (*Pause*)

INTERVIEWER   How long have you been writing these letters?

AGNES   Almost two years . . . You're not angry with me, are you?

INTERVIEWER   No.

AGNES   It means so much to her. It's important to her. It's something to hope for. You have to have something. People *need* something to keep them going.

INTERVIEWER   Do they?

AGNES   Yes. Sometimes I think, if we can wait long enough, something will happen. Oh, not that Mama will get better, but something . . .

So I write the letters. I don't mind. It's not difficult. I read little things in books and newspapers and I make up what's happening. Sometimes I just write whatever comes into my head. You see, Mama doesn't really listen to them anymore. She used to. It used to be the only time I could talk to her. But now it doesn't matter what they say. It's just so she knows that Claire is coming.

INTERVIEWER What happens when Claire doesn't show up?

AGNES Oh, but I don't think that will happen. I mean, Mama . . . well, she won't . . . I mean, even if . . .

INTERVIEWER You mean she'll probably die before she even finds out.

AGNES (*Nods her head*) Yes.

INTERVIEWER What will *you* do then, Agnes?

AGNES (*Surprised by the question, she looks at the* INTERVIEWER *for a long time. Then* . . .) It makes her happy.

INTERVIEWER Does it?

AGNES (*More confused*) I don't know.

INTERVIEWER What about you, Agnes?

AGNES Me?

INTERVIEWER Does it make you happy?

AGNES Me?

INTERVIEWER Yes.

AGNES (*She touches her head lightly.*) Please, I . . . I should be getting back.

INTERVIEWER Agnes?

AGNES Sometimes she does things now, I don't know why . . . I . . . (*Trying to accuse the* INTERVIEWER) The pain is much worse. This medicine you've given her . . . it doesn't help.

INTERVIEWER Yes, we know. It may be necessary to move her up to the hospital again.

AGNES But you said before . . .

INTERVIEWER I know.

AGNES And now?

INTERVIEWER It's hard to say.

AGNES No.

INTERVIEWER I'm sorry.

AGNES No, you are not sorry. You don't know. You put her in some room. You do one more operation. You wrap her up in your machines. You scribble on her chart. And then you go away. You don't know anything about sorry.

INTERVIEWER We hoped it wouldn't go on this long, but there's nothing we can do about it.

AGNES But I don't *want* it to go on. You promised . . . it can't! Even when she's asleep now, she has dreams. I can tell. I hear them. You keep saying, a few days, a few days. But it's weeks and months . . . all winter and now the spring . . .

INTERVIEWER She has a strong will.

AGNES (*Almost laughs*) I know that.

INTERVIEWER Sometimes that's enough to keep a very sick person alive for a long time.

AGNES But why? Why? When it hurts so bad? Why does she want to keep going like this?

INTERVIEWER She's waiting for Claire.

AGNES (*Stunned*) What . . . ? What did you say?

INTERVIEWER It's what we call "making a bargain." She's made up her mind that she's not going to die until Claire arrives.

AGNES (*Denying it*) Oh, no . . . no . . .

INTERVIEWER . . . it might easily be the reason. Now that you've explained about the letters.

AGNES . . . no . . . no . . .

INTERVIEWER AGNES . . . ?

AGNES . . . no . . . it isn't true . . . it isn't . . .

INTERVIEWER Perhaps it isn't . . .

(*In the cottage,* FELICITY *is slowly waking up. She mumbles.*)

FELICITY . . . Claire . . .

AGNES It isn't wrong to hope . . .

INTERVIEWER Agnes . . . ?

AGNES . . . waiting for . . .

FELICITY . . . Claire . . .

AGNES . . . no . . . she can't . . . she can't do that . . . she can't.

INTERVIEWER Agnes . . .

AGNES (*Rising*) No. Please. I have to go . . . I have to go back . . .

INTERVIEWER Listen to me . . .

AGNES No! . . . I don't want to.

INTERVIEWER Will you come back tomorrow?

AGNES Tomorrow?

FELICITY . . . put 'em away . . .

AGNES Yes . . .

FELICITY Put 'em away.

INTERVIEWER All right, then.

(AGNES *turns quickly and goes back into the cottage.*

The lights fade on the Interview Area.

At the same time, JOE *comes out of the cottage and goes to* MAGGIE *and puts a sweater on her shoulders.*

In the kitchen area, AGNES *goes to* FELICITY *and tries to comfort her disturbed sleep.*)

FELICITY . . . Claire? . . . Claire? . . . Claire?

AGNES . . . yes, Mama . . . I'm here . . . I'm here . . .

(*The focus shifts down to the porch area.*)

MAGGIE   I found a picture of us in New York. Kids. We were kids. Laughing. Standing on my head in Central Park. You were in uniform. What did we have? A few days in January was all. A little box camera, and that was broken, it didn't work all the time, you had to be so careful with it.

JOE   You were nervous all the time, you never stopped laughing.

MAGGIE   I was pretty in the picture. I had a head like a rock—headstands, handstands, cartwheels—Remember? I must have been crazy. I could run. I could sing . . . I was in the play one year. *The Red Mill.*

JOE   You got thrown out.

MAGGIE   I did not.

JOE   You got thrown out.

MAGGIE   No.

JOE   On your ass.

MAGGIE   All right, all right. It wasn't my fault. What was his name?

JOE   I don't know, Vice-principal, somebody.

MAGGIE   Son of a bitch kept putting his hands all over me. (*She almost laughs*)

JOE   You were pretty.

MAGGIE   I loved it.

JOE   You punched him in the mouth.

MAGGIE   I was scared. What else could I do?

JOE   You got thrown out.

MAGGIE   I got thrown out.

> (*The words spill as they remember bits and pieces of their life together, searching for some solid ground.*)

MAGGIE   I was still a virgin.

JOE   I never touched you until we were married.

MAGGIE I wanted you to. I did.

JOE Your mother would have killed me.

MAGGIE We went to New York . . .

JOE Sometimes Connecticut. With Steve . . .

MAGGIE He doesn't remember . . .

JOE In the fall, in the Plymouth . . .

MAGGIE I tell him, but he doesn't remember . . .

JOE Sundays and Saturdays, when I could get off . . .

MAGGIE He should have had brothers and sisters . . .

JOE We couldn't.

MAGGIE I know.

JOE They asked me all those questions. I was embarrassed, but I told them. They said, no, no more kids.

MAGGIE It hurt so bad, I cried . . .
    (*In the kitchen,* AGNES *begins to talk to* FELICITY, *who is still asleep.*)

AGNES Mama . . . Mama . . . ? Joes
    (FELICITY *continues to sleep.*)
  If I told you the truth, Mama, would you listen? If I told you the truth, would you think I was lying?

MAGGIE (*Continues with* JOE) . . . I cried.

JOE I built the house.

MAGGIE Way out in the country, we thought . . . way out . . .

JOE Something to *have,* we said. Where does it go?

AGNES (*Continuing to the sleeping* FELICITY) I don't remember the good times anymore, Mama. I keep thinking we have something to go back to. But I don't remember what it is. All I can remember is this . . .

MAGGIE What a house . . .

AGNES This . . .

MAGGIE Three bedrooms . . .

JOE One and a half baths . . .

AGNES   . . . pushing and pulling and hurting . . . this is all I can remember . . .

JOE   I did it all myself.

MAGGIE   The first two years, nothing worked.

JOE   What do you mean, nothing worked? I built it good, damn good.

MAGGIE   The wiring, the roof was bad, the plumbing, we never had water . . . (JOE *laughs*)

AGNES   It all went wrong. What happened, Mama? There must have been a time when I loved you. Oh, Mama, if I told you the truth, if I told you the truth now, would it matter?

MAGGIE   Then they put in the sidewalks, the sewers . . .

JOE   *They* never worked, either . . .
    (*They laugh.*
        In the living room area, MARK *is drinking heavily.* BEVERLY *enters from the bedroom where she has just left* BRIAN.)

BEVERLY   He's resting.

MARK   He'll be all right.

BEVERLY   How about you?

MARK   Better every minute. (*He downs another drink.*)

BEVERLY   You could fool me. (MARK *gives her a look.*) Okay, Okay. I'm going.
    (*She starts to collect her things.*
        In the porch area)

MAGGIE   More houses, more streets . . . You couldn't breathe.

JOE   Overnight . . . it happened overnight . . .

MAGGIE   We had to build fences. All of a sudden, fences . . .
    (*In the living room area*)

BEVERLY   You're sure he's all right?

MARK   Of course he's all right. It's just this dying business, Beverly. It gets a little messy every now and then.

BEVERLY   I noticed.

MARK   Did you? Brian takes such pride in putting things in order, keeping things in their proper perspective, it's hard to tell. I mean, give him ten minutes and a few thousand words, and he'll make you think dying is the best thing that ever happened to him. Would you like a drink?

BEVERLY   No, thank you.

MARK   It's all words for Brian. And it's a little hard to keep up. One letter follows the next, one paragraph, one chapter, one book after another, close parenthesis, end of quote. Never mind what it's all about.

BEVERLY   That's not fair.

MARK   Isn't it? The way you two have been carrying on, I was beginning to think I was at a wedding. I mean, I enjoy a good joke as much as the next fellow, but dead people are pretty low on my list of funny topics.

BEVERLY   Let's not get angry, we'll spoil your metaphor.

MARK   Fuck my metaphor! It's true! (*Pause. Then quietly.*) My God, listen to me. You think you know something. You think you *have* something . . .
     (*In the porch area*)

JOE   More houses, more streets.

MARK   And it all goes crazy.

JOE   So many goddamn things. Where do they go? The freezer, the washer and the dryer, a dishwasher for Christ's sake, the lawn mower, the barbecue, three bicycles, four, six lawn chairs and a chaise lounge—

aluminum, last forever—the white table with the umbrella, the hammock, the bar, I put that wood paneling in the basement, we finished the attic—well, half of it, I got the insulation in—the patio, with screens . . . ~~Jesus,~~ it was a lot to let go of.

MAGGIE   I don't want to talk about it.

JOE   Before you know it, everything you *had* is gone. Not that it was ever yours but you feel it anyway when it's gone.

MAGGIE   I'm telling you, I don't want to talk about it.

JOE   (*He turns from her*)   All right! All right! We won't talk about it.

MAGGIE   You get tired. You get old. My hands got too big. I got too fat. I don't know how it happens, I can't remember.

(*In the living room*)

MARK   . . . when I met Brian, I was hustling outside a bar in San Francisco. Right after the great "summer of love." You remember the summer of love . . . one of those many American revolutions that get about as far as *Time* magazine and then fart to a quick finish. Well, just after the summer of love, winter came. Which was the last thing anybody expected. And suddenly it got very cold. People were starving to death in the streets.

BEVERLY   Sounds lovely.

MARK   Very colorful—you would have liked it. Anyway, like everybody else, I was very hungry, very desperate . . . the whole scene. So there I was one night, like many other nights, ~~selling it~~ down on Market Street, I wasn't very good at it, but it was paying the rent, and Brian walks up to me . . . I didn't know him of course . . . he walks up and asks me the *time*. Right?

Well, I did my little number about time for what
and how much was it worth to him . . . I figured
anybody who'd come on to me with an old line like
that was good for a fast twenty.

And all of a sudden, he starts explaining exactly
what time *was* worth to him . . . Philosophy! On
Market Street.

And before I know it, he's into concepts of history,
cyclical and lineal configurations, Hebraic and Greco-
Roman attitudes, repetitive notions . . . time *warps*,
even! Jesus, I thought, I've got a real freak on my
hands!

BEVERLY You did.

MARK And he's talking and talking and talking and I'm
thinking I've got to score soon because it's getting late
and I need the bread and I'm hungry . . . but I can't
get *rid* of him. I walk away, and he walks away *with*
me. I go inside the bar and *he* goes inside the bar. A
real "fuck bar." I figured this had got to shake him.
Right? Nothing. He didn't even *notice*. People are
humping on the tables practically and he's quoting
Aristotle to me and Whitehead and elaborating on St.
Thomas Aquinas' definition of sin . . . completely
oblivious to everything around him! I thought I was
losing my mind. Finally, I said, "Look, man, I haven't
eaten in a long time, and I'm getting a headache. Why
don't we talk some business before I starve to death?"

BEVERLY What did he do?

MARK He bought me dinner! I couldn't believe it. I
mean, what the hell did he *want* from me? And he
never stopped talking. Never.

BEVERLY Perfect. And then he left.

MARK Right.

BEVERLY He didn't want *anything* from you.

MARK But before he went, I lifted his wallet.

BEVERLY   I always warned him not to talk to strangers.

MARK   It doesn't matter, because the next day I re-
turned it. I don't know why. I just did. And that's
how I got to know him. I got interested in what he
was doing . . . which as it turns out was nothing. But
he was doing it so well. He gave me a room. I could
use it whenever I wanted.

I started reading again . . . I thought to myself, my
God, I could really *do* something. Salvation! We
talked and talked endlessly . . . word equals idea
equals action equals change equals time equals free-
dom equals . . . well, who knows? But the point is
. . . What am I talking about?

BEVERLY   Dead people.

MARK   Exactly! I mean, exactly!

BEVERLY   Exactly what?

MARK   I mean *it's not enough!* Ten thousand pages of
paragraphed garbage . . . it's just words. We are
dying here, lady. That's what it's about. We are dropping like flies. Look around you, one word after another, one life after another . . . Zap. Gone. Dead.

Don't sit there with your ass falling off and try to
deny it. Because you can't.

Brian looks at me and I can see it in his eyes. One
stone slab smack in the face, the rug is coming out
from under, the light is going *out.* You can do the
pills and the syringes and the "let's play games" with
the cotton swabs and x-rays, but it's not going to
change it. You can wipe up the mucous and the blood
and the piss and the excrement, you can burn the
sheets and boil his clothes, but it's still there. You can
smell it on him. You can smell it on me. It soaks into
your hands when you touch him. It gets into your
blood. It's stuck inside him, filling up inside his head,
inside his skin, inside his mouth. You can taste it on

him, you can swallow it and feel it inside your belly
like a sewer.

  You wake up at night and you . . . and you spit.
You try to vomit it out of you. But you can't. It
doesn't go away. It stays inside you. Inside every
word, every touch, every move, every day, every
night, it lies down with you and gets in between you.
It's sick and putrid and soft and rotten and it is killing
me.

BEVERLY   It's killing him, too.

MARK   That's right, lady. And some of us have to
watch it. Some of us have to live with it and clean up
after it. I mean, you can waltz in and out of here like
a fucking Christmas tree if you want to, but some of
us are staying. Some of us are here for the duration.
And it is not easy.

BEVERLY   And some of us wouldn't mind changing
places with you at all.

MARK   And some of us just don't care anymore.

BEVERLY   What?

MARK   Some of us just don't care.

BEVERLY   You're cute, Mark. But next to me, you are
the most selfish son of a bitch I've ever met.

MARK   Oh, wonderful! That's what I needed. Yes, sir.
That's just what I needed.

BEVERLY   You're welcome!

MARK   Look, don't you think it's time you picked up
all your little screwing trophies and went home?

BEVERLY   Past time . . . way past time. The sign goes
up and I can see "useless" printed all over it. Let me
tell you something, as one whore to another—what
you do with your ass is your business. You can drag it
through every gutter from here to Morocco. You can

trade it, sell it, or give it away. You can run it up a flagpole, paint it blue or cut it off if you feel like it.

I don't care. I'll even show you the best way to do it. That's the kind of person I am.

But Brian is different. Because Brian is stupid. Because Brian is blind. Because Brian doesn't know where you come from or who you come from or why or how or even what you are coming to. Because Brian happens to need you.

And if that is not enough for you, then you get yourself out of his life—fast. You take your delicate sensibilities and your fears and your disgust and you pack it up and get out.

MARK That simple, huh?

BEVERLY Yes. That simple. A postcard at Christmas, a telegram for his birthday, and maybe a phone call every few years . . . if he lives. But only when it gets really bad.

When the money and the time and the people are all running out faster than you care to count, and the reasons don't sound as good as they used to and you don't remember anymore why . . . why you walked out on the one person who said yes, you do what you have to because I love you. And you can't remember anymore what it was you thought you had to do or who the hell you thought you were that was so god-damn important you couldn't hang around long enough to say goodbye or to find out what it was you were saying goodbye to . . . Then you phone, because you need to know that somewhere, for no good reason, there is one poor stupid deluded human being who smells and rots and dies and still believes in you. One human being who cares. My God, why isn't that ever enough?

MARK You want an answer to that?

BEVERLY No. I want you to get yourself together or get yourself away from him.

MARK Just leave.

BEVERLY Yes.

MARK I can't.

BEVERLY Why not?

MARK He's dying.

BEVERLY He doesn't need *you* for that. He can do it all by himself. You're young, intelligent, not bad looking . . . probably good trade on a slow market. Why hang around?

MARK I can't leave him.

BEVERLY Why not?

MARK I owe him.

BEVERLY What? Pity?

MARK No.

BEVERLY Then what? You don't make sense, Mark. I mean, what's in it for you?

MARK Nothing's in it for me.

BEVERLY So what's keeping you here? You said it yourself. He's just a tired, sick old man . . .

MARK What?

BEVERLY . . . A tired old trick with some phony ideas that don't hold piss, let one water . . .

MARK Get out of here.

BEVERLY A broken-down sewer, that's all he is.

MARK I didn't say that . . .

BEVERLY Yes, you did. Garbage. You can't even bear to look at him. You don't need that. You don't need to dirty your hands with that kind of rotten, putrid filth. Unless of course you need the money. What does he do—pay you by the month? Or does it depend on how much you put out?

(MARK *suddenly hits her in the face.* BEVERLY *quickly slaps him back—hard—several times.*
          MARK *is stunned.*
          So is BEVERLY.
          A sudden silence.
          Embarrassment.
          Pain.
          Finally, MARK *breaks down.*)

MARK   I don't want him to die. I don't . . . Please . . .
          (BEVERLY *goes to him tentatively and puts her arms around him*) I don't want him to die.
          (JOE *is at up left.* MAGGIE *is at up right*)

JOE   Maggie . . . ?

MAGGIE   (*Crossing to up left*)   I'm here, Joe, It's all
    right.

JOE   Maggie . . . ?
          (*In the kitchen area*)

FELICITY   Claire . . . ?

AGNES   Yes, Mama . . .
          (*The lines overlap, coming from all three areas.*)

MAGGIE   I'm here, Joe . . .

BEVERLY   It's all right . . .

FELICITY   Claire . . . ?

AGNES   Yes, Mama . . . I'm here . . .

MAGGIE   It's all right now . . .

BEVERLY   It's all right.

AGNES   It's all right . . .

MAGGIE   Sshhh . . .

BEVERLY   It's all right. It's all right.

MAGGIE   Sshhh . . .
          (*Pause*)

BEVERLY   (*Gently*)   Hopes, baby. That's what you got.
    A bad case of the hopes. They sneaked up on you

when you weren't looking. You think maybe it's not
gonna happen. You think maybe you'll find some way
out. Some word that's still alive, some word that will
make it all different . . . Maybe, maybe, maybe . . .

FELICITY (*Waking up*)   Claire . . ?

MAGGIE   It's all right . . .

AGNES   Yes, Mama . . .

MAGGIE   Sshhh . . .

BEVERLY   Please, baby. Just one favor you owe him.
Don't hurt him. Don't hurt him with your hope.
(MARK *pulls away from* BEVERLY) He needs somebody. (MARK *doesn't answer*) Yeah. That was my answer, too. (*She gathers her things.*) 'Bye, baby.

MARK   Wait . . .

BEVERLY   No, no. Another two minutes and I'll be
dancing you all over the floor.

MARK   I might not mind.

BEVERLY   Might not mind? You'd love it.

MARK   All right. I'd love it.

BEVERLY   Tell Brian goodbye for me.

MARK   Don't you want to see him?

BEVERLY   No. I've got a plane to catch. I want to get to
Hawaii before the hangover hits me. (*She stops and
turns to* MARK.) It's funny, he always makes the same
mistake. He always cares about the wrong people.
     (*In the kitchen area*)

FELICITY   Claire . . .

AGNES   What happened, Mama?

BEVERLY   Bye!

FELICITY   Claire . . .

AGNES   You sit down one day, and you get caught . . .
you get caught somewhere in a chair . . . in some foreign room. Caught in slow motion . . .

(BEVERLY *exits DL*)

stretched across the floor, listening to the windows and the doors. It's hard to remember sometimes what you're listening *for*. A whistle, maybe . . . or a shout . . . somebody calling your name. Or maybe just a few words. A few kind words. A ticket to Louisiana . . . a letter . . . something . . .

(*In the porch area*)

JOE A farm would have been nice.

MAGGIE We couldn't afford it.

JOE Some place all our own.

AGNES Something.

MAGGIE Just to watch the sunset?

JOE Every day a different job. Every day a different reason. Something grows, something . . . all in a day.

AGNES Something . . .

MAGGIE It would have been nice.

JOE Something to have.

AGNES Something . . .

JOE Jesus Christ, we built the house, and before we finish, fifteen years, and it's gone.

MAGGIE We didn't need it. It was more work to keep up than it was worth.

JOE Maybe . . . maybe it was. But it was *something*, wasn't it? Something to have. You put in one more fucking tree, you fix up another room, I kept seeing grandchildren.

What the hell else was it for? Not right away, but someday, you figure, kids running around, falling down under it, when it's grown big enough to climb and you can chase them down, spend some time running around the goddamn house . . .

MAGGIE (*Still detached*) The apartment is nice. It was closer to work.

JOE (*Starting to get really angry*) Work? Shit. Fifty weeks a year in a flat-wire shop. Twenty-four years.

MAGGIE We had the saloon in between. And the oil truck . . .

JOE A bartender and a truck driver in between.

MAGGIE We *owned* the bar. That was ours.

JOE Gone.

MAGGIE And the truck, we owned . . .

JOE All gone. Christ, even the factory is gone.

MAGGIE They couldn't get along without you.

JOE Twenty-four years. Two weeks a year at the beach. One week off for Christmas . . . (*Pause*) Talk to me, Maggie. Talk to me.

MAGGIE What? What can I say?

JOE I don't know. Somebody walks up one day, one day, somebody walks up and tells you it's finished. And me . . . all I can say is "what" . . . *what's* finished? What did I have that's finished? What?

MAGGIE We give up too easy. We don't fight hard enough. We give up . . . too easy . . .

JOE We got to tell him, Maggie. We got to face it and tell him. Some son of a bitch walks up one day and tells you it's finished. What? What did we have that's finished?

MAGGIE (*Breaking down*) Us. Us. For Christ's sake, don't make me say things I don't understand. I don't want to hear them. I shake all over when I think about them. How long? Two weeks? Three? A month? And then what? What have I got *then*? An apartment full of some furniture I can't even keep clean for company, a closet full of some old pictures, some curtains I made out of my wedding dress that don't even fit the windows . . . What? What do I do? Sit down with the TV set every night, spill my coffee when I fall asleep on the sofa and burn holes in the carpet, dropping cigarettes?

JOE Maggie . . . *put arms around*

MAGGIE *hit him* No. I want you to come home. What is this place, anyway? They make everything so nice. Why? So you forget? I can't. I want you to come home. I want you to stay out four nights a week bowling, and then come home so I can yell and not talk to you, ~~you son of a bitch~~. I want to fight so you'll take me to a movie and by the time I get you to take me I'm so upset I can't enjoy the picture. I want to make too much noise in the bathroom because you go to bed too early and I don't care if you *are* asleep because I want somebody, somebody to hug me once before I go to bed. I want to get up too early, too ~~goddamn~~ early, and I'll let you know about it, too, because I have to make you breakfast, because you never, never once eat, because you make me get up too early just to keep you company and talk to you, and it's cold, and my back aches, and I got nothing to say to you and we never talk and it's six-thirty in the morning, *every* morning, even Sunday morning and it's all right . . . it's all right . . . it's all right because I *want* to be there because you need me to be there because I want *you* to be there because I want you to come home.

hopes don't die

JOE Maggie . . .

MAGGIE Come home, that's all. Come home.

JOE I can't, Maggie. You know I can't.

MAGGIE No, I don't know. I don't.

JOE I can't.

MAGGIE You can. Don't believe what they tell you. What do they know? We've been through worse than this. You look fine. I can see it.

JOE No, Maggie.

MAGGIE You get stronger every day.

JOE It gets worse.

MAGGIE No. I can see it.

JOE Every day, it gets worse.

MAGGIE We'll go home, tomorrow. I got another ticket. We can get a plane tomorrow.

JOE Don't do this, Maggie.

MAGGIE I put a new chair in the apartment. You'll like. It's red. You always said we should have a big red chair. I got it for you. It's a surprise.

JOE No! It won't work.

MAGGIE We'll get dressed up. I'll get my hair done. We'll go out someplace. What do we need? A little time, that's all.

JOE It's not going to change anything.

MAGGIE No. It's too fast. Too fast. What'll I do? I can't remember tomorrow. It's no good. We'll look around. Maybe we *can* find a little place. Something we like.

JOE No. This is all. This is all we got.

MAGGIE No. Something farther out. Not big. Just a little place we like. *All right, a farm, if you want. I don't care. Tomorrow!*

JOE (*Angry and frustrated*) Tomorrow is nothing, Maggie! Nothing! It's not going to change. You don't snap your fingers and it disappears. You don't buy a ticket and it goes away. It's here. Now.

MAGGIE No.

JOE Look at me, Maggie.

MAGGIE No.

JOE *Look* at me. You want magic to happen? Is that what you want? Go ahead. Make it happen. I'm waiting. Make it happen!

MAGGIE   I can't.

JOE   Make it happen!

MAGGIE   I can't. I can't.

    (STEVE *comes out of the cottage.* MAGGIE *and* JOE *look at him.* MAGGIE *crosses away from* STEVE. *He speaks quietly, sensing that he's interrupted something.*)

STEVE   Hey, I'm ready to play for you now. If you want to hear?

JOE   Sure, dad. I'll be right in.

STEVE   It's not great, but it's not bad, either.

JOE   Good.

STEVE   (*To* MAGGIE, *tentatively*)   Mom, I'm sorry.

MAGGIE   What?

STEVE   I'm sorry for ~~fucking~~ around like that. I didn't mean to upset you.

MAGGIE   That's okay.

STEVE   Yeah?

MAGGIE   (*Smiles and goes to him*)   Yeah, yeah, yeah. (*She throws her arms around him and holds him tightly*)

JOE   You get tuned up, and I'll be right in.

STEVE   Better hurry up before I lose my nerve.

    (*He exits. After a moment he tunes up and we hear "Good Night, Irene" being played on the guitar*)

JOE   I'm going inside now, Maggie. I'm going to tell him.

MAGGIE   Tell me first.

JOE   What?

MAGGIE   Tell me. Say it out loud.

JOE   I'm going to die, Maggie.

MAGGIE   (*After a moment*)   Why?

JOE I don't know.
   I don't know. I don't know. Like everything else, I
   don't know. Come inside.

MAGGIE What'll we do in there?

JOE Try. That's all. Just try. Live with it. Look at it.
   Don't make me do it alone.

MAGGIE I can't promise . . .

JOE Don't promise. Just come inside.

> (MAGGIE *doesn't move for a long time.* STEVE
> *continues to play the guitar softly. Finally*
> MAGGIE *turns and walks slowly toward the cot-*
> *tage.* JOE *joins her and together they walk inside.*
>
> *As they pass through the living room,* MARK
> *checks his watch, rises from the couch and goes*
> *to the bookcase. He begins to prepare some medi-*
> *cine for* BRIAN, *but instead he picks up the tray*
> *with the medicine and throws it violently.*
>
> *After a beat,* BRIAN *enters.*)

BRIAN (*Looking at the mess*) What happened?

MARK Nothing. Nothing. I had an accident.

BRIAN Oh. Me too.

MARK What?

BRIAN I need some help.

MARK What happened?

BRIAN I . . . uh . . . I fell asleep and I wet the bed.

MARK Come and sit down.

BRIAN I'm embarrassed.

MARK I'm drunk.

BRIAN Pleased to meet you.

MARK Sit down. Before you fall down.

BRIAN (*Starts to sit, but then stops.*) I am truly dis-
   gusting.

MARK No, you're not. Just wet.

(BRIAN *reaches out his hand to* MARK, *they embrace. Then* MARK *helps him off to the bedroom. And our focus shifts to the kitchen.*)

FELICITY (*Calling out in her sleep*) Agnes.

AGNES (*Putting one capsule of the medicine into a cup*) Mama, if I told you the truth now, would it matter?

FELICITY (*Waking up*) Agnes!

AGNES (*When medicine is finished*) Yes, Mama?

FELICITY What . . . what time is it . . . ?

AGNES I don't know, Mama.

FELICITY . . . sons of . . . . . . Did we get any mail today, Agnes?

AGNES (*Every word of this lie is now more and more unbearable.*) Yes, Mama . . . we did . . .

FELICITY From Claire?

AGNES Yes, we did. Another letter from Claire. Another . . .

FELICITY (*As if she never said it before*) I get so lonesome for Claire . . .

AGNES (*Cutting her off*) I know, Mama . . .

FELICITY Will you read it to me, Agnes?

AGNES Yes, Mama.

FELICITY (*Like a phonograph, skipping back*) I get so lonesome for Claire . . .

AGNES (*Unable to bear any more*) Mama, please . . .

FELICITY I get so lonesome for Claire . . .

AGNES Please.

FELICITY I get so lonesome . . .

AGNES Mama. (*And then silence*)

FELICITY Agnes?

AGNES Yes.

FELICITY   Could I have some tea?

AGNES (*Pours the tea and carefully puts the cup in* FE-LICITY'*s hands*)   Yes.

FELICITY (*Holding the cup, but not drinking from it yet*)   Could you read me the letter, now?

AGNES   Yes.

FELICITY   The letter from Claire.

AGNES   Yes. Yes. Yes.

(*She takes the letter from her pocket—the one she was writing earlier. She opens the envelope and begins reading . . .*)

Dear Mama, I am writing today from Mexico. We are finally out of the swamp and onto high dry ground. What a relief after so much rain and dampness . . . Because of some unexplainable mechanical difficulties, we found ourselves stranded today in a beautiful little mountain village called San Miguel . . . It's a lovely little town clinging for dear life to the side of a great ghostly mountain in the middle of nowhere . . . a very curious place to be. Nothing has changed in hundreds of years and nothing *will* change, I guess, for hundreds more . . .

FELICITY (*Mumbling*)   . . . my bright-eyed . . . girl . . .

AGNES   . . . There are so many things to see during the day, but then the nights grow bitter cold . . . (AGNES *watches her, making up the words to the letter*) . . . and I can hear the wind blowing . . . outside the door, whistling and . . . and whispering . . . and when I look out the window, nothing is there . . . nothing . . . Mama . . . I think . . . I think it's because I miss you because it hurts not being close to you . . . and . . . and touching you . . . (AGNES *breaks down and can't go any further*)

FELICITY   Agnes?

AGNES   Yes, Mama. Yes.

FELICITY   What time is it now?

AGNES   Oh, four . . . five . . . I don't know.

FELICITY   (*Still holding her cup*)   Could I have some tea, Agnes? (AGNES *just looks at her*) Could you read me the letter now?

AGNES   Mama . . .

FELICITY   Could you read me the letter now?

AGNES   Mama . . .

FELICITY   The letter from Claire?
    (*Pause*)

AGNES   Yes. Yes. (*She starts to read the letter again*) Dear Mama, I am writing today from Mexico. We are finally out of the swamp and onto high dry ground. What a relief after so much rain and dampness . . . Because of some unexplainable mechanical difficulties . . .
    (*She continues reading under the following:*
      In the shadows, JOE *and* BRIAN *slowly become visible. They are standing in isolated areas, facing the audience as if they were speaking to the* INTERVIEWER.
    The coda music begins)

BRIAN   People don't want to let go. Do they? They think it's a mistake. They think it's supposed to last forever . . .

JOE   There's a few things—I could talk to you about them . . .

BRIAN   I suppose it's because . . .

JOE   . . . you don't expect it to happen.

BRIAN   You don't expect it to happen to you.

JOE   But it happens anyway, doesn't it? It doesn't matter what you do, you can't stop it.

BRIAN   You try.

MARK (*In the living room*) You keep thinking, there's got to be some way out of this.

BRIAN You want to strike a bargain . . . make a deal.

MARK You don't want to give in.

JOE You want to say no.

MAGGIE . . . no . . .

MARK . . . no . . .

BRIAN Your whole life goes by—it feels like it was only a minute.

BEVERLY You try to remember what it was you believed in.

MARK What was so important?

MAGGIE What was it?

BEVERLY You want it to make a difference.

MAGGIE You want to blame somebody.

BRIAN You want to be angry.

JOE You want to shout, "Not me!"

BRIAN Not me!

MAGGIE Not me!

FELICITY What time is it, Agnes?

AGNES I don't know, Mama.

BRIAN And then you think, someone should have said it sooner.

MARK Someone should have said it a long time ago.

BEVERLY When you were young.

BRIAN Someone should have said, this living . . .

MARK . . . this life . . .

BEVERLY . . . this lifetime . . .

BRIAN It doesn't last forever.

MAGGIE A few days, a few minutes . . . that's all.

BRIAN It has an end.

JOE Yes.

MARK   This face.

BEVERLY   These hands.

MARK   This word.

JOE   It doesn't last forever.

BRIAN   This air.

MARK   This light.

BRIAN   This earth.

BEVERLY   These things you love.

MAGGIE   These children.

BEVERLY   This smile.

MAGGIE   This pain.

BRIAN   It doesn't last forever.

JOE   It was never supposed to last forever.

MARK   This day.

MAGGIE   This morning.

BEVERLY   This afternoon.

MARK   This evening.

FELICITY   What time is it, Agnes?

AGNES   I don't know, Mama. It's time to stop. Please, Mama. It's time to stop.

BRIAN   These eyes . . .

MARK   These things you see.

MAGGIE   It's pretty.

JOE   Yes.

MARK   Yes.

BRIAN   These things you hear.

MARK   This noise.

BEVERLY   This music.

STEVE   I can play for you now. It's not good, but it's not bad either.

MAGGIE   Yes.

BEVERLY   Yes.

BRIAN They tell you you're dying, and you say all right. But if I *am* dying . . . I must still be alive.

FELICITY What time is it?

MARK These things you have.

MAGGIE Yes.

JOE This smell, this touch.

MARK Yes.

BEVERLY This taste.

BRIAN Yes.

MAGGIE This breath.

STEVE Yes.

MARK Yes.

BRIAN Yes.

MAGGIE Yes.

BEVERLY Yes.

JOE Yes.

BRIAN This moment.
　　　　　(*Long pause.*
　　　　　Lights fade.)

Telador

Bigger Brief

More physical on Felicity

funny on Gardenia.